MOMS ON CALL

Toddler Book

Laura Hunter, LPN and
Jennifer Walker, RN, BSN

Moms on Call – Toddler Book
Copyright © 2012 Jennifer Walker All Rights Reserved
Revised 10/2021
Printing 6

Printed in the United States of America
ISBN 978-0-9854114-1-1

Editing by Tim Walker, Morgan Eddy and Elizabeth Moyer
Cover photo by Alice Park Photography
Cover design and logo design by Kristen Smith and Alice Park
Family photo on back cover by Alice Park Photography

Published in the United States by
Moms on Call, LLC
5200 Dallas Hwy Ste 200 #226
Powder Springs, GA 30127

"This book is dedicated to the living God that guides our paths and makes every day an exciting adventure"
— Jennifer and Laura

(Left to right: Laura Hunter, LPN and Jennifer Walker, RN, BSN)

About the Authors

Laura Hunter, LPN

Laura is a juggler—she juggles life (can you relate?). She is a mother of five, pediatric nurse with over 20 years of experience, an entrepreneur, and a highly sought after infant care consultant who has an international following. But there's one common passion for all the areas of Laura's life- her desire to inspire and encourage parents.

Jennifer Walker, RN, BSN

Like Laura and most other moms today, Jennifer has multiple roles—wife, mother of three, pediatric nurse, public speaker, sought-after infant and toddler care consultant and author. Jennifer has over twenty years of pediatric nursing experience and has a heart to equip parents with practical advice and inspiration for the joys and challenges of parenthood.

Moms on Call, LLC is an Atlanta-based phenomenon. We
started serving local families with in-home parenting consultations from birth to 4 years of age. And now, by combining technology, common sense and a passion for families, we have supported and partnered with parents all over the globe. Our books, swaddling blankets, online resources and seminars are all available at www.momsoncall.com.

Seeking medical care whenever you are concerned is recommended by Moms on Call.

Any time that you are concerned, or notice any symptoms, call your pediatrician's office. Sometimes toddlers have discreet symptoms like a fever, and other times there is just something that you can't explain; call it mother's intuition or a nagging feeling that something may be wrong. Those are both valid reasons to seek medical attention. Many of the concepts addressed in this book vary from pediatrician to pediatrician. When it comes to your child's care, you are responsible for making the final decisions.

This book is designed to provide information on the care of toddlers. This book is intended as a reference volume only, not as a medical manual. It is sold with the understanding that neither the author nor the publisher are engaged in rendering medical, health, or any other kind of personal professional services in the book. The reader should consult the services of a competent pediatrician, registered dietician or other medical professional. The author and publisher specifically disclaim all responsibility for any liability, loss, or risk, personal or otherwise, to any parent, person, or entity with respect to any illness, disability, injury, loss or damage to be caused, or alleged to be caused, directly or indirectly, of the use and/or application of any of the contents of this book.

The book should be used only as a supplement to your pediatrician's advice, not as a substitute for it. It is not the purpose of this book to replace the regular care of, or contradict the advice from, the American Academy of Pediatrics, or any pediatrician, nutritionist, registered dietician, or other professional person or organization. This text should be used only as a general guide and should not be considered an ultimate source of childcare, child rearing, discipline technique, child feeding, food preparation/storage, or as the ultimate source of any other information. You are urged to read other available information and learn as much as possible about childcare and the nutrition and feeding of young children. Mention of specific companies, organizations, or authorities in this book does not imply endorsement by the publisher, nor does mention of specific companies, organizations, or authorities imply that they endorse this book.

Every reasonable effort has been made to make this book as complete and as accurate as possible. However, there may be mistakes, both typographical and in content. Therefore, this text should be used as only a general guide. You should discuss with your pediatrician the information contained in this book before applying it. This book contains information only up to the copyright date. New information, or information contradicting that which is found in this book, should be actively sought from your child's competent medical professionals.

Testimonials

"It's so concrete and doable! 'Yes, ma'am and DO it.' Don't ever get discouraged. If you can make a know-it-all pediatrician feel empowered, just think what you're doing for people who have no child development experience." - Tammy W.

"This information was so informative and helpful, especially at clearing up things I wasn't sure how to deal with, and addressing some of the things I currently use that don't seem to work. I have read a number of parenting books in the last year to try to sort through this toddler phase and assumed that most books and courses offered the same information. Your resources, however, was definitely a practical 'here's how' that even addressed things like faith and character building. Thanks again for all you all do at MOC! It is literally making a difference for people across the globe."
– Lizzy

"Landon is 14 months old now and I can't believe it. He's a totally different child since this past May when you came into our lives!" - Kimberly H.

"We have really had a life-changing experience with our kids! Riley Jane is sleeping through the night and not crying! They are much better over all and both teachers at school even made a comment!" – Meredith H.

"Y'all are truly amazing! I wanted to let you know that you were dead on with the potty training. Hamilton was potty trained (and happy the entire time!) right at his 2nd birthday. It's been a dream. And you were right— go straight for the underwear! Thank you!" – Jaclyn A

"We implemented the three family rules. We then backed them up when Jacob would come out of his room after being tucked in. We did have two rough nights when he tried to knock down the door, but it has been great since then. He no longer comes out of his room at all and sleeps all night! I am totally convinced that the enjoyment (and number of hours of sleep we're all getting) of being a parent is in large part due to your advice—knowledge is power!" – Andy S.

I cannot even believe what a turn around we have made. I really didn't think my son would ever sleep again!! But he has been sleeping again 11 hours a night and a two-hour nap every day. He has not told me once in the entire last week that he doesn't want to go to sleep. He has not cried, thrown a temper tantrum, or gotten out of his crib!!! As for his testing behaviors, I am using the tools you gave me and we have had a big success in a short time. I also haven't had to use time out in over a week as the threat of it now stops the behavior. Thanks again! "- Brett

"Thank you for the humor, understanding, and solid advice that you provided." – Angela P

"If I had known it would go this well after only a week, I would have done this earlier" – Tracy T

"I have been recommending the Moms on Call materials to all my friends and I have been getting feedback that they love it and that it works!" – Bethany W.

Table of Contents

FOREWORD

I will never forget the day that Laura Hunter told me that she was pregnant with twins. In those moments of sheer elation and blinding fear, a friendship was forged that would change our lives forever. Laura already had two children, a lovely teenage daughter and a towheaded precocious toddler.

We had worked together for over a year, since I had come back to work after the birth of my own twins. I was busy managing life with the three children. We leaned on each other a great deal over the next year. There were calls each day as encouragement spilled from one phone call to the next.

We worked at a busy pediatric practice in North Atlanta as after-hours nurses and our job was to field several hundred phone calls each week that came in at all hours, day and night. We split the responsibilities, giving us a chance to be moms and to serve the great patients that sought out counsel, medical advice and the understanding voice of another mom.

We had a great friendship and we were managing our busy schedules. I had my angelic mother-in-law who taught me fierce loyalty to God and family and watched my children while I worked, but Laura and Jim had to manage their four kids all on their own. However, it was not long before the surprise of the decade occurred and Laura was pregnant with number five, and shortly after "Little Handsome" was born, our story begins.

Dr. John Knox called Laura into his office to chat about the challenges of being 'on-call'. They agreed that it would make a huge difference in the lives of new parents if they just had someone to go to their house and help them to figure out what to worry about and what not to. He predicted that it would cut down on the bulk of the calls to the office and it did.

Parents often asked about what to do with fussy babies, sleeping and feeding issues and basic concerns straight through to toddlerhood. It was then that he looked Laura in the eye and told her that she should start to see our patients in their homes and help settle them into parenthood. Of course, Laura was on-call 90 hours a week, had five children (including a newborn) and was barely sleeping herself as she managed the on-call hours five nights a week.

But something he said resonated in her heart. She came to me to flesh out what home visits would look like and what kind of information should be shared. So, we wrote a little folder of information that we knew new parents needed and off she went into the first few households, armed with a folder that we printed off our computer.

What we discovered in those first days, were parents that were so exhausted and anxious, it was difficult for them to fully enjoy their precious babies. So, we put together everything that we knew would help babies to sleep and organized the schedules that followed a baby's normal sleep/wake cycles. What happened next amazed us.

We received email after email from parents that put these concepts into practice and had households with happy babies. It was not just a few emails but EVERY SINGLE client that we visited with these principles responded the same way. We were flabbergasted and in disbelief, and we knew that we were on to something.

We met for coffee shortly thereafter and as women of faith, we prayed about what to do next. We had this vision of moms begging for help, wondering why things were so difficult, wanting to get some rest and know how to care for their babies and toddlers with confidence.

It was then that we put these principles in a book to outline all of the helpful techniques that promoted great rest.

We, also, organized the decision-making process we used when we took calls at the office in a simple and easy to follow format. After doing a consultation for Kenny Rogers, (who copyrighted our book and helped us get set up on the Internet in response to the increasing demand for our materials), things really took off. Our first book, *The Moms on Call Guide to Basic Baby Care: 0-6 months* was picked up by a national publishing house and was translated into three languages and went through six printings!

Word of mouth grew our business 600% in the first two years. We were doing consultations for families all over the United States and picking up our first consults out of the country. Our methods have been used all over the world. And as our business grew, so did our client's children! So back to the drawing board we went and developed no-nonsense principles for toddlers. Who knew that night waking, bed sharing and three hour long evening battles were at epidemic proportions around the country? When we expanded our services to include children up to five years of age, we exploded again.

The most satisfying moments were (and still are) getting the emails from families who had once been broken by exhaustion and frustration but discovered the effective methods that would change the entire atmosphere of their household. The process was more difficult the older these children became; but when these families followed the principles, their lives were changed. A full night's sleep is a precious thing and such an integral part of a healthy household and healthy children. But we went beyond that, using discipline methods that helped during the daytime as well. Addressing every concern from potty training to the "no" stage.

But the biggest thing that parents, moms especially, wrote to us to tell us that they appreciated was the tone of our materials. It has always been intensely important to everyone at Moms on Call to deliver advice with encouragement and truth, not guilt or fear. We recognized that many of the messages that moms were receiving through many other channels were implying that they were not good enough and not doing it right. That is not OK with us. And one thing that you will find in our materials is that we support parents, we believe in parents and we want parents to feel confident in their decisions (whether they do it the Moms on Call way or not).

From 25 years of pediatric nursing experience and children of all ages (and sizes) came some of the most appreciated advice from moms to moms (and sweet dads too)! The principles that we cover in this book are forged from personal experience and years of having the privilege to partner with parents as they manage the joys and challenges of toddlerhood.

This book is dedicated to the parents who work hard each day raising their children, wading through all of the mountains of information available and trying to make clear choices. Our hope is that we have provided a resource that is accessible, practical and contains truths that will resonate with parents everywhere. Let's get started!

LESS FRUSTRATED MORE EFFECTIVE

Psalm 90:14
Oh, satisfy us early with Your mercy,
That we may rejoice and be glad all our days!

Reality Parenting

With my first son, I remember thinking, "*Why would anyone even consider raising their voice to discipline? This is a breeze.*" He was a little over two at the time and was a late bloomer in the 'free-will' department. Honestly, he was the first everything; grandchild on both sides and nephew to five doting adults. Life was full of attention for him and I thought I had it all together. (If you are rolling your eyes right now, we understand.) But I was not out of the woods. His challenging years hit around age three, just in time for his twin brothers to be born, and I immediately understood all too well the reason moms wanted to raise their voice— sometimes just to be heard! (-Jen)

The good news is that this is not a promotional resource for yelling at your children. In fact, we are going to learn a lot about how to stay in control and avoid the situations that make us want to scream, shout or pull our hair out. But in order to get there, we have to address a few things that stress us unnecessarily. And at the top of that list is the idea that we can and should be perfect parents.

At Moms on Call, we like to fill our resources with good news and here is the first of many: there is no such thing as a perfect parent! We liken them to unicorns—we have always heard they exist, but we have never seen one. Oftentimes, parents find themselves trying to function as if perfection is the only option to successfully raising a healthy, well-adjusted toddler. We constantly compare ourselves to this non-existent ideal while trying our best to keep our little secret. We are not perfect, regardless of what the pictures on social media imply.

We hope that the following statement will not scare you away, but we have to tell you: _this book will not make you a perfect parent._ If that is what you are looking for then put this down right now. We'd love to take you on a journey into the very real place where neither the toddlers nor the parents are perfect, but they are genuinely less frustrated and enjoying more of life together. It's a place that we live in each and every day, a place called "reality". So, if you are still reading, then take every lingering fantasy of some 'fashionista' mom leisurely walking behind a stroller (in heels), balancing a latte in one hand while reading the unabridged encyclopedia to her angelic faced (listening) toddler dressed in matching (and unstained) layers of adorable clothing with socks and shoes INTACT—and throw that idea in the nearest hypothetical ditch.

If you are willing to lay down the fantasy of perfection and embrace the unpredictable roller coaster that is toddlerhood, we can move forward. We are all parents with different temperaments and life experiences raising toddlers with different temperaments in different life situations. Just because another parent has a mild-mannered child, does not automatically make them a better parent than you; and it does not make them perfect. So, if your friend has a child that can recite the constitution at age three and your son farts for laughs, they can both be successful adults (although the farting kid is going to have a bit more fun along the way).

So, agree even now to lay down that unrealistic perfectionistic expectation of yourself so that we are free to address the real life situations we face each day; like what to do when a 'little someone' starts throwing the sippy cup off

17

the side of the used stroller (with food smashed into every crevice), and we can't even find the shoe that was once firmly planted on that chubby little foot. Ah, here we are in the real world. It is refreshing to know that there is hope in the land of missing socks and shoes!

Now, that we have decided that parenting perfection is a pipe-dream (say that three times fast!), we can begin to work on becoming more successful, less-frustrated parents. I know some of us are still having trouble letting go of that elusive dream of perfection, but rest-assured that we will feel like better parents when we understand how our toddlers learn and communicate and when we lay down the ineffective, time-consuming and frustrating ways that we have been trying to get through to them. Want to have more time and energy to devote to enjoying your family? Read on.

SUM IT UP

o   There is no such thing as a perfect parent

o   Parenting is not about perfection; it is about perspective.

o   There *is* such a thing as a less frustrated and more effective parent (let's go there!).

The Modern Generation

One of the most important ways that we can make more time in the day and decrease our frustration is to unload some digital-age habits that are not helping us. You know the ones that we are talking about. When you were on the computer late at night and you entered "fever and rash" into a search engine only to lose sleep for a week over what turned out to be heat rash and a broken thermometer.

We are a culture like none other. Our parents learned how to diaper a baby by watching their moms do it. We can learn how to diaper a baby by watching YouTube on our smart phones (thanks Moms on Call!). In fact, long before we ever had a baby, we started researching the Internet with the fervor of a scientist vying for the next Nobel Peace prize. We enthusiastically filled our shelves (or e-readers) with 10-12 baby books and started following the blogs of 200 complete strangers and all of our friends with kids. And some of the stuff we read, made us laugh, some made us cry and some of it made us very afraid.

Then as our children grew, we settled into a time of feeling pretty confident. And before that had a chance to really sink in, they graduated into toddlerhood and we were faced with having to research yet again. But this time it wasn't just "fever and rash" but "discipline and tantrums" that were being typed into our search engines. Then, we quickly discovered that there were many ideas and opinions out there and that they could be passionately opposed to each other, polar opposites. So, the places that we went to ease our heart and teach ourselves about parenting turned out to be a huge maze of opposing ideas; each one with its own "studies" and "data."

19

Parents have access to more information than ever before in history. Yet, we have to ask ourselves: "Has that helped or hindered our search for parental sanity?" It doesn't take long to discover that the result of information overload is not enlightenment, but confusion.

In fact, there is one phrase that can turn a normally sensible parent into an anxious ball of mush. It's the phrase "studies have shown." There was a time when those words were dependable. But to us, the most marketed-to generation ever to walk the planet, we know that people can get "studies" to say anything they want.

As pediatric nurses, we could not even get three doctors to agree on what type of cold medicine they like to use, much less agree on the finer nuances of child-rearing.
Parenting resources are some of the worst offenders. One book may condone a certain discipline method and another insists that very same method will lead to the creation of a social deviant.

How do they say that with certainty? Well, studies have shown..... Really? What studies? Can I read them? How many children were studied? Who paid for the study? The truth can get hidden in the rhetoric and the average parent barely has time to take a shower much less research statistically significant study results on the Internet.

Can we find reliable directions on the information highway that will give us an accurate picture? Of course we can. We are smarter than our smart phones.

There was a time when parents did not have access to endless talking heads or 'scientific' results and the most unbelievable thing happened—they parented anyways.

Could it be that parental intuition is still available? **Could we make some decisions straight from the proverbial "gut" and still maintain credibility with our play-group?** The answer is a resounding "yes." We can throw out the notion that in order to make parenting choices, we have to back up each of our decisions with "Well, studies have shown…" Let's ask a different question. What does my common sense tell me? Can I stand up for the decisions that I make completely on their own merit?

You are the one who has watched your children interact and grow. You know when they took their first step, how wide their grin can stretch, the exact color of their sparkling eyes and the challenges they face. You have more information about your child than any scientist, anywhere ever did. So, you are, by far, even without the input of the entire 'world wide web', best able to make choices on your child's behalf.

Don't be frightened. Give it a try. You may find that it makes life easier and gives you a surprising amount of confidence. Then, before you know it, the power of the phrase "studies have shown" will no longer trump your inner parent.

And the result of that will be that this generation of toddlers is not going to be raised by Google searches, psychologists, television personalities or even "experts." They are going to be raised by parents. They are going to be raised by you! And you are completely capable of making solid decisions of their behalf.

As goofy as this will make you feel, say this aloud:

"I am the parent." Give it some attitude.
"I am the PARENT." Yes, you are, honey. Yes you are!

You are the parent. As parents, we have the privilege of taking credit for the crowning moments and taking responsibility for the mistakes. And if we do that, then we are well on our way to making solid choices and being an example of a well-grounded, well-adjusted adult who can take care of a toddler (or two, or three!). _We are not perfect, but we can adapt, we can learn and we can become more effective and less frustrated parents._

It helps to limit the amount of information that we allow to affect our most important life decisions. This will make us considerably better decision makers all by itself. And before we know it, our decision-making abilities will seem less cumbersome and more natural.

Social Media
Another big influencer that has a profound impact on our generation is the recent explosion of social media. Social media has created another new parenting style, **parenting by popular opinion**. Why not? I mean we have access to hundreds of complete strangers, good decision makers... or not (there is no way to know).

Which is one of the reasons that it is not advisable to ask your 450 Facebook friends what they think about letting your toddler cry in "time out" for five minutes.

You will get a few responses including but not limited to:
- The guy friend who has a slightly humorous take on the situation.
- Another mom who says something like "time out never worked for us."

- Someone who brings up the phrase, "You do know that studies have shown....."

So, therein lies your panel of experts and you are no closer to feeling confident about your decision to put little Ethan in time out for drinking out of the dog bowl— again.

The problem with "popular opinion" is that it changes dramatically and frequently. Parenting by popular opinion is like stepping off your porch with your eyes closed and trying to see if you can use the wind to direct you to your mailbox. It is not a dependable way to get from here to there but it *is* a dependable way to get lost and become really confused.

Select a few friends that you trust who have children who seem basically normal and well behaved and ask them about your parenting challenges. Just a couple of well-seasoned parents with multiple children will give you a greater sense of where to go with that time-out than 450 strangers or a host of research scientists.

Dads
Now that we have talked about a few modern voices that are *not* helpful in our quest for parental sanity, let's discuss one that is. In our generation, we often leave behind one of the most important parenting voices in our child's life, the voice of the dad.

We hear moms say that they often feel that dads are too harsh. "*He didn't read 15 articles, four parenting books and search the internet for two days! How is he supposed to know what he is talking about?*" Although, Dads are not always the ones to read parenting books (but some do and love it!), they actually have a great, untainted sense when it comes to parenting.

What we have seen time and time again, is that parenting intuition comes more naturally to those who limit the number of voices and opinions that weigh in on their final choice. **The ones who choose wisely, a few people or resources that they trust make better decisions and feel better about the decisions that they make.** It just so happens that many dads do just that. They are good at it. So, let those dads weigh-in on parenting decisions.

The other thing that dads provide is balance. A father's strength can hold up our weakness and vice versa. And when a child sees that in action, they begin to realize that their dad can help them to be strong too. (Moms are strong in other areas, valuable ones; hear our hearts here.)

If you find yourself saying *'he just doesn't understand what I am going through'.* He may not, they do not always feel things in the same way that we feel them, but they do feel. They love in different ways and that is a good thing. You will be a stronger parent when you work together. And if you are a single parent, you are exactly as strong as your child needs you to be.

To sum it all up, we avoid taking advice from people who do not have a vested interest in our child's wellbeing. The truth is that we will make mistakes and we will also knock some choices out of the ballpark, but we will make those decisions, every last one of them.

Even as you read through these resources there are parts that will resonate with you and seem to jump off the page. There will be things that will align with your personal experience and some things may seem foreign. Embrace what resonates with you. You are the parent. You get to decide. You are good at this.

SUM IT UP

- o Try parenting by what you know, not by what you Google.
- o The ones who choose wisely, a few people or resources that they trust, make better decisions and feel better about the decisions that they make.
- o Popular opinion changes every few months, your spouse does not. Discuss parenting decisions with your spouse instead of your Facebook friends and you will change your mind less often.

Can I Get A Job Description?

Now that we have unloaded some modern habits that were stressing us out. Let's move forward and figure out what we can do with all that time we are saving.

What is the role of parent really? Is there some happy medium between the eccentric families depicted on reality TV and the dreamy, perpetually smiling, well-dressed family that graces all of the furniture commercials (the ones with children playing on a white couch without getting it dirty— as if that ever happens!).

In order to explore the true job description of a parent, let's cover a few things that it is not. There are two very common categories that apply to many of us. The first of these being:

THE FRIEND ZONE: This was an unwanted place to be in a dating relationship, and is an equally unwanted place to be in parenting. Many of us are afraid to discipline our children because we fear that if we do, they won't like *US*. However, that undermines the very healthy authority relationship that will help our toddlers face real life. They do not typically like the correction, but they will love the one who is dependably in charge.

Besides, our children will have many friends to fill that role, and those friends will come in and out of our houses eating up all of our snacks. So, that role is not beneficial and it's taken. Which brings us to the second common role that does not serve us well, which is:

THE GRANDPARENT ROLE: The parent that dons these sensible shoes has one thing on their mind—making the child happy at all costs and making sure the noise level stays down. Now, don't get us wrong, this sounds like a really fun job and we hope to get there one day; but it is years down the road when our grandchildren are born.

There are times that toddlers will have a full-blown tantrum, and they will try to get their way through creative manipulation tactics. However, someone has to stay in control when our toddler's emotions are spinning out of control. **Giving in to each demand is just a sure-fire way to raise a demanding and rarely satisfied child.** So, we cannot fill the grandparent role—maybe someday, but not today.

We cannot leave the ever-important essential role of PARENT unfulfilled. It would be like careening down a hill in the car with no one in the driver's seat, scary and unpredictable for us all.

When we seek to fulfill the "FRIEND" role or the "GRANDPARENT" role, we are placing all of our focus on our children to determine how we should respond to every situation. It is a pressure that they feel and do not know how to handle.

Households will work best when the focus is on the household as a whole, when we have a "family" schedule and when we take into account what is best for the running of the entire household—mom, dad and other siblings included.

Life was not meant to revolve around one child. But as loving and attentive parents, we often find ourselves stressed out because ***we are constantly trying to make life accommodate our children instead of making children that can accommodate life.***

When they learn to accommodate the realities of life, they are happier and have a sense of confidence and accomplishment. Being in a family, like being a part of a community, requires the ability accommodate others, which is ultimately a source of true joy.

Living in a family, also, takes some self-control and our toddlers have more than we think! They are much more resilient than culture would lead us to believe. And at the head of every family is a unique and imperfect creature called a parent. And who is the parent?
_ __ __ ____! Yes! You certainly are.

The role of PARENT is both challenging and wonderful. Parenting "experts" agree on few basic truths but this one is something to which everyone can agree: parenting is essential to a child's health and well-being. So, as a parent, the one uniquely designed to be in control, we must ask ourselves "If we are not here to make sure that our child is happy every second of the day, then what are we supposed to be doing?"

Well, one thing is for certain, we are not here to shield our children from every challenge that they face or protect them from the normal patterns of life. We are here to teach and equip them to *manage* the normal patterns and challenges of life. We keep the structure of life intact so that they can learn to grow and thrive and interact with the world in which we live. We are in the business of **life preparedness** not conflict avoidance.

There are enough regular challenges simply built in to everyday life; learning to eat and sleep, welcoming a sibling into the household, going to school, changing teachers and moving to a different town—just to name a few. We do not have to go looking for these things; they will find us. Our job is to provide a positive and dependable structure so that they can adjust. And to be their biggest fan, the first one that ever believes in their ability to conquer life's challenges.

You know what makes the challenging times of life so much better? Having someone dependable by your side to guide you through it and believe you can do it! That is what our toddler really wants from us. We can do that by being consistent, trustworthy teachers. So, let's break this down a little bit:

Consistent: we want to be as consistent as reality allows. None of us are going to handle every infraction with confident ease, but we are going to have a dependable structure in place that helps our children understand what we want from them in clear, well-defined ways.

Trustworthy: We want our children to know that we mean what we say and that we will do what we say we are going to do. It gives them great security to know that we are reliable. We reveal our character to our children in the way that we deal with their behaviors. Let us put it like this—when my child's friends are planning an all-nighter and want him to sneak out of the house, I want him to say to his friends, "You don't know my mom, bro, she does what she says she's going to do and I am not risking that for nothing." (Although a part of us would want him to say it using proper English, we'll take it just like it is.)

Teacher: Let's get beyond, "No" and teach them some alternate behaviors. Toddlers are not going to come up with effective coping mechanisms all on their own. Let's just give them some good options. So read on as you embrace your role as PARENT. The consistent, trustworthy teacher is in us somewhere!

SUM IT UP

o Someone has to stay in control when a toddler's emotions are spinning out of control (easier said than done but we'll teach you how!).
o What makes the challenging things of life better? Having a consistent, trustworthy teacher by your side to guide you through it and believe you can do it!
o We get more satisfying results when we go beyond "No" and teach them some better options for behavior.

It Is All About the Atmosphere

We are so excited about this next section because within these pages you will find some more of that extra time we promised and unravel why living with your toddler feels so frustrating at times. We want you to feel less like your toddler is a ball of drool, destruction and drudgery and see them more often as a ball of excitement, exploration and sheer joy. We are getting there!

What is "atmosphere"? We are so glad you asked. Atmosphere is the familiar way that your household works. In my childhood home, I watched my parents treat my grandparents with love and respect – every time they visited. Therefore, my household had an atmosphere of non-optional love and respect for grandparents.

Do you know what this means? It means that we can have a household with an atmosphere where the adult is in charge, in a loving and sensible way. We are going to teach you how to make this the familiar way your household runs.

We can take control of the whole atmosphere and stop communicating to our toddlers over and over that we are at the mercy of their 3-year-old decision-making capabilities. I would get increasingly frustrated when I would recognize that all day, I ran around trying to "convince" my 3 year old twins to do what we needed to do next. They did not always want to go potty, get in the car or eat breakfast. I thought that I just needed to find a way to explain it to them better. What I really needed was some tips on how to communicate that I was in charge. What it took some time to realize is that some things in life are non-optional and enforcing that is a normal, healthy way for a household to work!

We often live in an atmosphere where the toddler is in control of when and how things happen from feeding to nighttime sleep. That is a HUGE responsibility for such a young child and they do not have the capacity to make reasonable decisions at this age.

There is not a recorded moment in history when a loving parent explains that it is time to finally leave the indoor play area because it has been . . .
-a very long stay
-we have run out of tokens
-the birthday party is over
-everyone else is leaving now
-if we don't leave right away its going to get too late
and our babysitter who is at home with the baby will be wondering where we are.

And after that five-minute attempt to explain WHY it is time to go, the toddler responds "That makes perfect sense Mommy, let's leave this carnival of goodness; strap me in that car seat and take me right home, I can't stand it when I stress out the babysitter!"

The great news is that they do not need all those explanations, just a simple non-optional direction will do. "It is time to leave, we are going to start our engines and get out of here" and then ...we leave (toddler in hand, possibly screaming) but lovingly and confidently, we are out the door. We will discuss more on this, later in this resource (like in the cheat sheet section at the end so you can get the short version when you need it).

32

For now, we are going to reveal those secret communications that have been going on, right under our noses, without a second thought that have been communicating that the atmosphere in our homes has the toddler in charge. These are the things that undermine our entire parenting experience. And a few time-outs or an occasional spank is not going to "fix-it," and it is not going to put us in charge.

The great news is that communicating to toddlers is actually easier than we think. We are going to change the way that we communicate and start to comfortably set ourselves in the role of parent, the reasonable decision maker who has this thing under control and in so doing, we will set an atmosphere in our homes that life works best when adults are in control. When we communicate simply, clearly and confidently, we get much better results. So, keep reading, things at your house are about to get a whole lot easier.

The most important thing to do to transform your household is to set the overall atmosphere. We have more power to influence the atmosphere of our households then we can imagine.

Taking control of the atmosphere will help you enjoy the company of your toddler and decrease the escalating frustrations in the day. The communication habits of the modern-day, loving parent that unknowingly undermine our effectiveness as parents are:

- o Asking too many questions
- o Using the word "OK" at the end of non-optional statements
- o Over-explaining.

Asking too many questions sets up an atmosphere that nothing can progress in the day without a toddler's PERMISSION.

We simply are in the habit of asking toddlers too many questions about the non-optional events of life. Does this sounds familiar? Do you want to go upstairs for a nap? Are you getting sleepy? Do you want the door opened or closed? Do you want Mommy to sing 5 songs, read 7 books, lights up or down, red sippy cup or blue?

Households run better when the older, smarter one is in control. Naptimes, feeding times and sleep times are <u>non-optional events</u> that will proceed for the good of the household and the good of the toddler, whether they choose every detail to their exacting (and often changing) specifications or not. This will make things run much smoother. For the *non-optional* events of life, avoid too many questions and start giving clear directions.

What toddlers really want are 2 pieces of information:
     1. What is happening.
     2. What you want them to do about it.

So, this is simple. Try this on for size.
"It's naptime. You are going upstairs for your nap and you are going to be great at it!"

The first few times that you start this, we can actually catch that little ball of energy unaware and they just do it. However, do not be discouraged if they do not get up, thanking you for your clear direction and waltz themselves to their room, closing the door and turning off the light on their way to dreamland.

o   Ask questions less and give directions more.
o   Reserve questions for optional events and play.
o   Households run better when the older, smarter one is in control (that's you!)

The second thing that undermines our overall daily routines is saying "OK?" after non-optional statements.

Putting "OK" at the end of non-optional events sets up the atmosphere that we cannot proceed without a toddler's APPROVAL.

We are going to potty now, OK? It's time to leave for school, OK? Put your socks on, OK? Hand me that sharp knife in your knife in your hand, OK!?

In the adult world, the term "OK" means, "Do you understand what I am saying?" In the toddler world "OK" means "We will only proceed with your approval." We inadvertently imply that we require their approval for every step of the day and in so doing, drive ourselves bonkers.

Needing a toddler's approval for every activity of the day sets us up for chaos. Putting "OK" at the end of a sentence makes the statement a *request*. A common scenario is saying to our toddler, "It's time to have lunch now, OK?" And the toddler is thinking *"Thank you for asking but actually I am having a great time with my toys at the moment."* And then we respond by repeating our _optional_ statement three or four more times, getting more irritated when our toddler is not responding to our _request_.

So, from here until preschool, let's make a change that will help our little ones know what to do next. "It's time for lunch and you'll be great at it". Then take them to the table for lunch with a smile.

It can be difficult to drop "OK?" off the end of our sentences. Which is why we try to make it as easy as possible. Simply try replacing "OK?" with "You'll be great at it".

- Clear direction (followed by action) gets better results than waiting for a toddler's approval.
- Replace the "OK?" with "You'll be great at it".
- Setting up an atmosphere where the adult is consistently in charge takes time; go easy on yourself (oh, and you'll be great at it!).

And the final modern habit that undermines the atmosphere of our households is over-explaining. Over-explaining sets up an atmosphere that we cannot proceed without a toddler's COMPLETE UNDERSTANDING.

It is fine to explain how the train tracks fit together or how to dress a Barbie doll (even though Barbie's arms do not bend!). But when it comes to getting in the car for school, we want to avoid setting up the atmosphere that we need their complete understanding before we proceed out the door. Because we would have to wait until they reach elementary school age to get it!

Toddlers are making decisions solely on the basis of what feels good at that moment. They do not choose what is "best" for them because it makes "sense". That is what they want us to do *for* them.

The trouble with over-explaining is that we are asking something of a toddler that they cannot developmentally handle. It can take precious time out of our packed day to try to "reason" a toddler into the car. They may respond to a confident face and love the attention, but they do not respond to reason.

So, avoid going into a long diatribe about the day that looks something like this "Don't you want to go to school today and see Jordan? He is going to be wondering where you are. If you are *late* Jordan might begin to *worry*. And if we don't get in the car right now, there will be *traffic* and we will have to wait in the long line... and on ....and on ....and on...."

How about we save some time each morning and decrease the frustration by just saying: "Time to get in the car for school, let's start our engines and get outta here!" No explanations, no coaxing, no other options, no gauntlet of five decisions to make. We are getting in the car and that is the only option.

Toddlers respond best by having a parent that is CLEAR, CONFIDENT AND IN CONTROL.

We simply tell them what it is going to happen and how they should respond. "**We are getting in the car now, let's start our engines and get outta here.**" When we communicate in that way over and over, they will catch on. It creates the atmosphere that the adult is in charge. Can you imagine feeling like you are actually in charge of the daily routine again? It is possible. You can do it!

So, no more over-explaining; kiss the hours of coaxing and convincing good-bye and become a clear communicator! Toddlers do not want explanations and they do not want to make three hundred decisions each day. They want clear direction and they want to know that someone in the household is confident and knows what to do.

Who's the parent? _ _ _ _!

Setting up an atmosphere where the adult makes the decisions is much like travelling by ship. Let's say that I am travelling to Greece on a cruise ship. I want to be free to enjoy the ride and take advantage of all the fun activities, but I cannot do that if I am the one in charge of steering, mapping out the route, navigating the storm or deciding which way to turn every four minutes.

I want a captain to do that so I do not have to worry about it. I want to have someone dependable, that I trust to be taking care of all of that; someone who has been on the water before and knows the ship inside and out. That is what the toddler wants. **Steer the ship so they can enjoy the ride.**

Do not worry. It takes time to steer the boat in a different direction. Extend grace. Remember to set aside fun-time where you can ask questions and explain stuff. There is a time for those things. We want your toddler to learn and engage and answer questions in a laid back and fun setting when it is not undermining the flow of the whole day. Having clear direction for all the **non-optional activities** in the day will buy you that fun-time and give you the presence of mind to enjoy it.

- o   Be free! The day will run smoothly without a toddler's full understanding of every move.
- o   Steer the boat.
- o   Setting aside fun playtime where you can explain things to your hearts content will give you the satisfaction of teaching in a gratifying way.

Confident Face

There is more to effective communication than just words. Toddlers are like little CIA agents. Their ability to read a situation is unmatched. They are watching our FACES. They study us from the day they get here and are tuned in to our patterns of behavior. Therefore, we are going to practice some "Confident face." It is a face that says, "We are getting in the car, there are no other options." In doing so, we establish an atmosphere of confidence and loving authority, because **a confident face is a powerful tool**.

Toddlers base their reactions on our reactions. And sometimes, they are simply dramatic and no matter how calmly you handle the normal spills of life, they will cry like they are trying to win an Oscar! Either way, calm and confident parental reactions tend to send the message that you are in control and that is exactly what a toddler wants to know, even if they are freaking out.

Part of developing confidence is completely buying in to the truth. When you commit to a truth like, "My child can get in the car in the morning without a fight and be great at it" then you are much more effective at communicating that truth.

Some of us need more practice than others; some of us self-doubt ourselves into making a continuous stress-face. We may constantly doubt if we are doing the right thing and it produces stress-face. Or we may be so tenderhearted that any negative behavior from our children stresses us so badly that we feel that we cannot hide our concern.

Many of us (moms especially) place unnecessary eternal significance on our toddler's every moment. We somehow believe that something as simple as enforcing a reasonable bedtime, mishandling a fall at the playground or not forcing enough vegetables down their throat will ruin them for LIFE.

This makes us have the "I am burdened with the *forever-ness* of your every move" face. We have a minute-by-minute rundown in our minds of how guilty we should feel about every perceived action (been there!).

If there were sports announcers echoing our real thoughts, it might sound something like this:

"Bulking up for the big game but Noah is not eating enough veggies again, he will grow up deficient and it will be ALL MY FAULT. Where is he going now folks? Oh to the bathroom to play in the toilet but not actually poop in it because he will be going to college in a diaper and it will be ALL MY FAULT. Oh, it's a clear foul in the back forty as Gillian tackles her classmate, she may never adjust socially it will be ALL MY FAULT. "

Sound familiar? Sounds like constant stress face is inevitable.

So let's address the forever-ness. Let it go. Lay down the forever-ness just for today. Give it a try. Try to be in the moment. You are going to like it so much and feel much more free to enjoy your life with your children. Take a deep breath and do this exercise for the next 24 hours.

Lay down the forever-ness and pick up the now-ness. Deal with the behaviors in the moment as they pertain to day-to-day life. It will help you to have a much more confident face, it may even bring an unexpected smile at the end of the day and the stress of parenting will ease up considerably.

Recognize that the big things that you provide are a safe and loving environment for this little one to learn and grow. You have the big things covered and they are much more indicative of what this child will do when he grows up than how many bites of broccoli he ate when he was three years old. (Their taste-buds mature as they get older, by the way—which is why we don't have a ton of toddlers drinking coffee. Thank God!)

No matter what the underlying cause of the faces we make during the day are, the great news is that confident-face is a skill that can be learned! (And just so you know: I was such a people-pleasing, tender-hearted, ball of gush that it took me a good while to develop the confident face that communicates the truth to my children -Jen).

We can make clear statements all day long, but if we say it with the "concerned eyebrows" then we are not convincing anyone, including our toddler. Ok, now it is time for the awkward exercises.

We want you to practice making clear statements in the mirror. Or better yet, invite over a close friend and practice together. It is a fun and silly time with outstanding results. Do not skip this exercise.

Take as much time practicing "confident-face" as you need. Your tone should be nonchalant and matter-of-fact, as if you know, so completely, that your child is able to do what you are instructing them to do, that their immediate reaction doesn't bother you.

Let's take 'getting rid of the paci' as an example. As they adjust to life without the paci, there may be screaming and pleading. But it meets the same confident phrase every time; "You don't need the paci anymore and you are going to be just fine". That statement is true, clear and can be repeated 100 times over. And after about three days, confident face has won out and they move on (no permanent, irreversible side-effects at all- just no more paci).

Your confidence is contagious. We are turning the tides and instead of having toddlers that set the atmosphere, we will set the atmosphere. We will take our household back for the sake of everyone's sanity and we will run the show. You can do this! And they will love it!

The atmosphere that we are going for is CLEAR, CONFIDENT and IN CONTROL.

In order to establish that in our households, we need to be aware of their developmental limitations and then actually believe that they can do what we are asking them to do! The power of that statement can change your household all by itself. When you believe it, you can communicate it simply and confidently. When you can communicate it, they can respond to it. When they respond to it, they begin to have confidence in themselves!

These are the tools that are going to help us run each day with greater efficiency, enjoy our toddlers more and keep clear boundaries in place.

Now, many of you are thinking that repetitive confident statements are not going to work as my toddler clobbers his brother with the plastic baseball bat. And you are right! We are going to take these communication principles and apply them to misbehaviors in a very organized and helpful way.

Even when we improve our communication skills, our words and confidence can be lost on a little one. We have one more very important tool in communicating with a toddler and that is ACTION. We will put action behind our clear, confident words.

SUM IT UP

- o Use "confident-face" and a "matter-of-fact" tone.
- o Toddlers want someone who is clear, confident and in control.
- o Live in the moment. You will love it!!

The Positive Truth

We are several important steps closer to freedom from wanting to pull out all our hair! One of the biggest reasons that we are feeling so trapped by our toddler's behavior is because of our biggest parenting challenge; our old nemesis, fear. Trying to parent out of fear is like trying to run a 10K with a six-ton ball and chain attached to your ankles. You can't go anywhere and you are exhausted!

If that sounds like your household (and we all end up here at one time or another), then read on because we are about to overcome more stuff that keeps us tired and stressed!

The most helpful tactic of an effective parent is to **parent out of truth and not out of fear**. This is a crucial determination if we are to free ourselves to parent with confidence. When we are making decisions on behalf of our children, we are going to learn to stop and ask ourselves three questions.

- o Am I making this decision out of truth or fear?
- o What is the truth in this situation?
- o How can I act on that truth?

Every situation that produces stress in your household can sit under the canopy of these three questions.

Try a few of your own. Take those things that you have been putting off in regards to parenting and break it down to the most essential truth.

Examples:
- o My child can learn to speak to me in a respectful manner without whining.
- o My child can sleep all night in their own bed.
- o My child can hold my hand when we cross the street.

They can! They can! They can! But they may not believe it until you do first. Once we have established the truth in any given situation is the first step in placing that truth firmly in the heart of our toddler.

Then the atmosphere of the household changes entirely. Instead of reacting to the toddler's fickle and often exaggerated responses to life, we establish the truth and help *them* to recognize that truth with clear, confident repetition. **So, they are not in control of how we feel about life, we are in control of how we present life to them.**

Therein lies a crucial step to changing their behavior. We begin to believe in the truth with everything within us, then we say it in clear, confident, and repetitive statements (peppered with love) and finally, we ACT on that truth.

Be patient, it takes a toddler time to catch on but they will! This is not a "have a perfect toddler in a week" scheme, this is a lifestyle that helps produce good things in the hearts of our children in the long run.

We have learned that truth does not lie on the other side of a computer screen or hidden in the pages of the latest baby magazine or even in the mixed, dramatic responses of our toddlers; it lies in the heart of the parent. Many of us are afraid that we do not have it. But it is in there and some days we will have to cling to it for dear life.

SUM IT UP

- Truth lies in the heart of the parent
- Parent out of truth, not out of fear.
- We want to *prepare them* for life in positive ways, not save them from it.

FREE WILL VS. BOUNDARIES

Psalm 16:6
The boundary lines have fallen for me in delightful places.
Indeed, I have a beautiful inheritance.

Myth of The Perfectly Behaved Toddler

The toddler stage is unlike any other in the life cycle. They are different than adults, they are different then babies and they are even different than early elementary-age children. Earlier we dispelled the mythical creature called the perfect parent. Now we are going to tackle the elusive offspring of the mythical "perfect parent" which we will call the "perfectly behaved toddler."

We have already recognized some important things about the ways toddlers think.
- They do not respond to reason.
- They cannot process abstract ideas.
- They are literal (when we put "OK" at the end of a sentence, they take that literally).
- They cannot follow long explanations.
- They want clear direction and the sense that someone confident is in control.
- They want someone to believe in them.

We cannot make perfectly behaved, robot toddlers. The toddler season is one of testing and trying. It is the time when they begin to acclimate to the daily routine that we put in place for them, testing each boundary along the way.

One concept that helps us to face the toddler years is to recognize that toddlers misbehave. Some will test their boundaries more than others regardless of how beautifully they are parented. What we are going to learn to do is to manage and handle the misbehaviors in ways that teach and equip our children to deal with the realities of life.

Another way to decrease parental frustration is to recognize that **your toddler's behavior is not an indication of your self worth**. Being less concerned with what people will think about *you* when your child misbehaves and concentrating more on the opportunity that you have to teach your toddler how to appropriately behave will foster a freedom that produces additional strength to manage the challenging moments.

Speaking of freedom...when your toddler's free will shows up, life does become more challenging, inside the home and out. This is normal stuff! So, let's talk about free will.

In the toddler years, this new skill surfaces; the recognition that they can make decisions about things. They would like to explore this new skill and learn how to wield it. This process is similar to the time that they learned to walk— wobbly at first, then more and more steadily they circled the living room looking to us to help them navigate the safest path. And we proudly covered table edges and fireplace corners with soft, industrial plastic and finally put that antique glass coffee table in the basement.

We made our home a safe, dependable environment in which they could learn to walk. We set up boundaries so they would not trip down stairs or get out the door into the street before they knew to look both ways!
So, when free will shows up, it is a new skill just like walking and we help set up a safe environment so they can learn how to manage it.

They get to make some smaller decisions, like which activity at the playground to ride first. And we continue to make the big decisions—like what time they go to bed, how they are allowed to treat us and even a few life-style choices such as how to clean up the toy store that landed on our living room floor.

In short, great parents have toddlers who misbehave sometimes as they navigate this new skill called free will. As a Consistent Trustworthy Teacher, your job is to teach them that their choices have consequences. Some consequences are good and some are not. The ones that are not will put a blip on their conscience so that they recognize what behaviors are not acceptable.

We help them manage that free will, teaching good options along the way. **We teach our child how to respond to our authority and when it is clear, consistent and dependable—they feel safe.**

SUM IT UP

- We cannot make perfectly behaved toddler robots.
- Your toddler's behavior is not an indication of your self-worth.
- Good parents have toddlers who misbehave.

Accidental vs. Defiant

Now that we have discussed that all toddlers misbehave to some degree in order to test their boundaries, it is time to learn what to do about it. First, there are two primary behaviors for a toddler:

1. Accidental
2. Defiant

Accidental behaviors—like crying when they fall—is a reason for simple instruction. "Wow, you were running faster than you thought. Try walking up to your cousin for a hug." But a toddler who looks you in the eye while doing something they know is wrong is exhibiting 'Defiant Behavior'.

You know the look. You know that they understood that you said, "Do not touch grandma's antique lamp" and they paused, got closer to the lamp...closer... and then touched it and looked right at you with a "so there" look on their sweet, little face.

And that defiant face awakens a frustration in us. We sense that a challenge has been made, and it has.
When your child looks you in the eye and does a defiant behavior they are saying, "Give me a boundary. Are you in control?"

Sometimes defiant behavior starts at 13 months, sometimes it stays dormant until they are 2 or 3 years old. When your child looks you in the eye and does a defiant behavior then it is time to start to get serious about the dependable boundaries in their lives. Because **the safest place to learn how to manage this budding free will is within clear boundaries that stay in place.**

Here is another key element to understanding your toddler. Every toddler wants us to provide one important thing in life and that is SECURITY.

It is the one thing that a toddler needs but will not tell us. Toddlers have little true control over what is happening in their world. Therefore they are in a fierce pursuit of security. Security is the one thing that a toddler will spend a majority of their time trying to establish.

SUM IT UP

o Testing boundaries with defiant behavior is a way for a toddler to get reassurance in how the world works.
o Although it does not seem like it, toddlers want boundaries and they want those boundaries to be predictable.
o We can help them to feel SECURE by keeping boundaries in place.

The Beauty of the Boundary

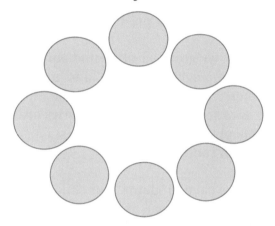

Boundary Stones

Keys to Character Building

This is a concept that was derived from an ancient people called the Israelites. As they wandered through the desert thousands of years ago; they would stop to make camp. They would surround the camp with boundary stones so that the people would find security in knowing that it was safe within the boundary of the stones.

Within that circle, things were familiar and predictable. They were free to learn and grow and interact. There, they had a safe place in which to develop, thrive and learn. This is similar to what our children desire from us. They want boundary stones that are kept in place. **They want a**

familiar and dependable place where they are safe to learn and explore.

When we think that our parenting efforts are not effective because they still misbehave, we are mistaken. They are just testing the boundary to see if it is still there. They want to know that this place called 'home' is where they are safe, secure and things stay relatively the same. That means the boundary stones stay in their predictable places.

For instance, when we go on vacation and our sleep boundary stone is moved because the kids (understandably) stay up late; when we get home, they will run into some of the other stones to see if the other boundaries are still in their predictable places. This is how they establish that life is again secure and in control.

This is also why we have to "detox" our children from grandma's house. In wonderful grandmotherly style, her house does not have the same boundaries that ours does. When the kids get home, they will test the home boundaries and even throw a few tantrums trying to establish that this is still the dependable place where boundaries stay in predictable places. Bedtime is still seven thirty, they still cannot eat ice cream for breakfast and they still cannot push their little brother. Ahhhh, this *is* home, now they feel secure.

Our challenge as confident, trustworthy teachers is to recognize that our job is not to move (or remove) every boundary that makes our child unhappy. It is simply to keep these boundary stones in place

Boundary Stones

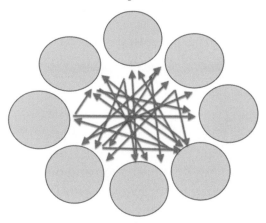

Keys to Character Building

A toddler's job is to constantly run into the boundary stones to reassure themselves that they are safe and life is in control. If the boundaries predictably stay put, then they will run into them less and less often and feel comforted and secure more often. If we keep moving the boundaries because they seem to "not like it," then they will test the other boundaries with greater fervor trying to establish some order and consistency.

As we said earlier, **it is OK to get your toddler to do something that they do not like to do.** That is a very healthy life-style that all of us are subject to. In order for life to run smoothly, we have to get in the car, wear seatbelts and get the rest that our bodies need—even when life is filled with distractions and endless entertaining alternatives. The way to truly enjoy play time and exploring time is when the structure of life is held solidly together within stable boundaries.

Boundary Stones

Keys to Character Building

We are going to discuss these boundaries in greater detail; but before we do, let's get to the nitty-gritty. How are we going to keep any boundary in place? You may be able to think of a few boundaries that you would like to put in place right now. And yours may look slightly different, but these are a great starting point.

SUM IT UP

- o Toddlers test their boundaries to meet their need for security.
- o Our job is to keep those predictable boundaries in place even if they seem to run into them often.
- o It is OK to require your toddler to do the things that are good for them, even when they do not like it.

_____

_____

_____

BRINGING OUT THE BEST BEHAVIORS

Hebrews 11:1
Now, faith is the assurance of things hoped for, the conviction of things not seen.

Hearts Open for Instruction

So how are you doing so far? Are you ready to put dependable boundaries in place? Excellent. Even now, you may be noticing that a new, more hopeful parent is emerging. So, let's put all of these concepts into practice as we learn when and how to address our child's misbehaviors.

Let's talk about the "when" - the times that a toddler's heart are open for instruction.

We are going to cover three times that we can place something valuable in our child's heart. Two of them are easy and fun, and the third is challenging but completely necessary. We have to use them all together to get the maximum effectiveness. These are outlined in the "Cheat Sheets" section in the back of this resources as well. We put it all together there for the busy parent on-the-go. That will give you time to concentrate on these simple techniques without having to worry about how to put it all together. Take your time. Take some deep breaths. You are about to learn how to make order out of chaos and communicate the things that you really want your toddler to know and feel.

The three methods of affecting a child's behavior and keeping clear boundaries in place are:

- o   Meeting between awake and asleep (fun)
- o   Triangulation (fun)
- o   Three Point Teaching technique (not so fun)

Between Awake and Asleep

See if you can fill in the blanks:
Jack be nimble, Jack be quick Jack ____ ____ __ _ ____
_____!
Humpty Dumpty sat on a wall, _____ _____ __ _ ____ ___.

When we were children, it was popular to read nursery rhymes right before bed. And we still remember those words spoken to us when the stimulation of the day had come to a close. We get a *short* (and I emphasize *short* – as in, under 3 minutes) window of opportunity to place something very powerful in their little hearts right before bed. Right in those few minutes between awake and asleep.

Between awake and asleep, we have a chance to communicate the thing that will influence their behavior more than any 'time out' or 'count to three' ever did. We have the chance to communicate that we believe in their ability to do what we are asking them to do. And instead of it being "us against that irritating behavior," it is "us supporting them through that behavior".

We are going to launch our crusade of simple truth and support on a solid foundation. So, at the end of the day, when the stimulation of the daytime activities has settled down, we will put something very valuable in that heart of theirs. We will begin to make order out of chaos. We will acclimate them to the first three boundary stones, the simple structure that will serve them and the household for the rest of their days.

Three Household Rules

To effectively make order out of chaos, we have to, first, establish order.

The toddler's mind is a unique place and it cannot categorize large amounts of information. That is why we have three household rules. And those three, easy-to-understand, household rules will be our first boundary stones.

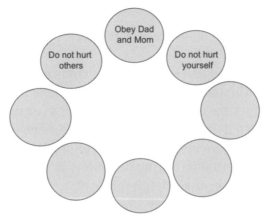

Boundary Stones

Obey Dad and Mom

Do not hurt others

Do not hurt yourself

Keys to Character Building

Often in our households, we have so many rules that the toddler cannot remember and categorize them all.
- o   Don't touch the stove.
- o   Don't disturb daddy when he is on the phone.
- o   Don't run into the road.

- Don't throw your toys.
- Don't pee in the Home Depot parking lot.
- (And just for parents of boys like ours) Don't hit your own self in your own head with your own foot! (Long car ride—enough said.)

There are just too many rules. We can keep track, but they cannot. They are just trying to sort out a few colors and put together a sentence! So we want to narrow the list to three rules that they can understand and those are:

- Obey Daddy and Mommy
- Do not hurt yourself
- Do not hurt others.

This is simple and all of the other rules can fit into one of these categories. As we said, the time that we place this in the heart of our child is right before bed or as we mentioned earlier, what we like to call "between awake and asleep."

We like to say it like this:
"We have three rules in this house and they are: Obey Daddy and Mommy, do not hurt yourself and do not hurt others because we are Walkers and Walkers are good to people."

Insert your own name into that scenario and choose a character trait that defines your family. Go over these rules each night, right before bed. This is not the time to go over the history of good behavior, just the three household rules, short and simple.

As your child grows up and opportunities arise to do the wrong thing, there will be a truth planted deep in their hearts that will serve as a reminder and level of protection. It could very well play out like this: "The other kids were making fun of that little girl but I did not do it because I am a Nelson and Nelsons are good to people." The nighttime routine will be covered in more detail in a later section but the important thing here is to always carve out that little 2-3 minutes of time between awake and asleep and set a sure foundation in your child's heart.

Once your toddler can start filling in the blanks, i.e.
"Obey Daddy and who?"
"Mommy"
"That's right!"
Then we can start addressing behaviors. We will first mention something that they did well, a time they followed one of the household rules. Then, once their heart is pried open a bit further with that positive input, we make a short, clear statement about the behavior we are working on together. It will look something like this:

1. Three household rules
"Obey Daddy and Mommy, do not hurt yourself, and do not hurt others because you are a ___ and ___ are good to people"

2. One thing they did great:
"I love how you obeyed Mommy and stopped throwing toys when I told you to stop. Way to obey Mommy!"

3. Then the thing we are working on:
"And today, you pushed little Freddie at play group which hurt him and we do not hurt others. Now, I know you can treat Freddie nicely. **You'll be great at it. You will figure it out**."

Our three minutes are up—conversation is over. We just placed ourselves on his side. We believed in the truth which is that he CAN learn how to treat others well.

Tomorrow he may push Freddie again; but, over the next few nights, we will communicate that we believe in his ability to do what we are asking of him. It is a powerful tool. It will not work all by itself but it is a healthy way to start to put these behaviors on their little radars and help them to manage the unwanted behaviors that they all exhibit at one time or another.

This time before bed will be a time to meet with your children for as long as they reside under your roof. A sweet time that will become the highlight of your day.

Every night, within reason (date night is the night we skip it!) we will be repeating this process. It may seem mundane at times but keep it up! We are not covering a laundry list of unwanted behaviors, just the one thing that is most important to us, or causing us the most frustration.

If it is hitting another child at school we may mention how he can treat others with kindness for a solid week at night. Don't worry; we will use other ways to affect their behavior as well.

Now, meeting these munchkins right before bed for a few minutes is fun and relatively easy but it is the long game that makes the difference. Do it nightly, start even before they have words (12-13 months is not even too early) and it will be a great way to transition the "Tender Time" of infancy into a connection time that will grow with them through toddlerhood. (My twin boys wanted to rough-house until the last second before bed, and I remember praying that I could just make it through one book without them trying to eat it or rip it. This was when they were two years old, but we still managed to squeeze in the rules and the few positive statements even if they were barely listening at first. It will get better. -Jen.)

If you have multiple children, it is fine to do this exercise nightly with all the children in the same room and then separate them out (if needed) to their respective sleep environments.

SUM IT UP

- o For the first week, just work on saying the household rules each night.
- o Then, make a short list of behaviors that you are working on in this order
  1. Sleep issues
  2. Feeding issues
  3. Things that frustrate you in order of importance to you.
- o Practice how you can say things as an encouraging statement (i.e. "Today you peed in the yard, but you are going to get the hang of getting that pee in the potty where it goes. You will be great at it.")

Triangulation

Another way that we will help our toddler to want to behave is to use the way they are wired. They long to impress and please the people that they love. So use triangulation to encourage them. Triangulation involves you, the child and someone they love or respect.

We want to be noticed and we want to be encouraged. Our toddlers do as well. And we can utilize this concept to put good behaviors on our toddler's radar. We help them become interested in good behaviors by communicating to others that they can do it.

Take potty training for instance. One of the ways that we will put this skill on their little radar is to "talk them up" in front of the people they care about. So when grandma comes over to babysit, you say to her:

'Micah and I were working on potty training today and he is going to be great it. He is totally going to figure this thing out." Again, the face is confident and the tone is matter-of-fact. We do not go over the history of indoor plumbing or gush as if we just won the lottery. We just make a confident statement of future fact to someone our toddler loves while our toddler is in earshot.

Use the child's name when you talk about them, always build them up with a positive appraisal. What we want to communicate here is that you are confident they are going to get the hang of this. Now, his reputation in front of dad, grandma or a favorite babysitter matters, and it is beckoning a successful poop in that potty.

If sleep time is your biggest challenge, then at the dinner table, make sure to point out that your child can do it. "Bill, I cannot wait for the night when Peyton closes her eyes, pulls up her covers and goes right to sleep! She is really going to get the hang of it. She is such a great kid." Make sure to say this when your child is in earshot (do not say it directly to your toddler at this time). They love to hear us praise their good behavior in front of the people they love and admire.

However, this concept also rings true with negative comments. As moms, clearly, we have some tough days and we want to unload and explain our feelings to other adults. We presume that our child is not really 'listening'. Do not fall into that trap. They are paying attention and if we tell people how bad our toddler has been and how they are never going to learn to behave, our child may begin to live up to our expectations. It is perfectly normal to reveal our fears and frustrations to our spouse or close friends, just keep those conversations to private times.

Here at Moms on Call, we are about having a right hand line and a left hand line and functioning somewhere right in the middle. When our children do accomplish the thing that we have been working on, it is best to have a satisfied demeanor. The message we are getting across is, "I knew you could do it." We do not need to hold a ticker tape parade when our child poops on the potty, sleeps all night or eats their food. We don't want to take this method to the extreme.

We can celebrate their accomplishments. We just want to have an air of confidence about it. Think of it like this. Do you do your best touchdown dance when your husband eats his food or goes potty? (If the answer is yes then that is one fun household you live in!)

"You did a great job. I knew you could do it." A wink, a big smile and a proud demeanor will go just as far as a full-on dance routine of gladness.

This does NOT mean that they can "do no wrong." We are about to learn a great incident-specific three-point teaching technique that will address the unwanted behaviors that reside in every toddler. We will also catch them between awake and asleep and go over the things that we need to work on at that time. Remember, these methods are meant to be used together.

But if you are working on a specific behavior like getting your child to sleep all night in their room, tell their loved ones how great they are going to be at doing just that—even before we have evidence that it is true!

SUM IT UP

- Speak things that are not as if they ARE. "Brantley is going to sleep all night in her new room like a champ"
- Do not overdo the triangulation because toddlers are bright and they will be on to us. 2-3 times a day is the maximum we want any one thing mentioned.
- It is fine to celebrate but try not to overdo the celebration. No need to get the poms-poms out with every bite of veggies.

Three-Point Teaching Technique

Now we come to the portion that is the cure for all that shouts: "I mean it! I really mean it!" (Loosely translated by every toddler, ever, as "I have five more minutes to continue whatever I am doing.") They know that if you really meant it, you wouldn't have to say it.

One of my favorites is a phrase my mother said when I was growing up. We lived in the sweltering heat of the Florida sun and had very heavy sliding glass doors that led to the backyard. When I would, lazily, leave the glass door 2 inches open, my mother would yell
"What are you trying to do, air condition the whole neighborhood?"

To which I would reply (silently in my head), "That would be fantastic! It's hot out there!" (-Jen)

When trying to deal with our toddler's frustrating behaviors, we make many an empty threat and allow our toddlers to watch as the colors of our face turn six different shades of pink. **Most of what drives up our blood pressure is related to the fact that we do not want to discipline them when they clearly need it**. It is all discipline avoidance on our part.

We are frustrated somewhat by their behavior and even more frustrated with ourselves because somewhere deep inside, we feel that we needed to intervene 2 ½ minutes ago (or for some of us 2 ½ months ago) but did not. The reasons are understandable. It is often because it is hard to discipline, we are not sure what to do or we are afraid of doing the wrong thing. With that in mind, the following information is aimed at making this easier.

As parents we usually do not have a problem saying "No." although oftentimes our child responds by grinning mischievously as if "No" is a game. The littlest Hunter child mistakenly thought that his last name was "No.". Making him "Brent No" because he was in to everything and heard it so much! (– Laura) Most of us recognize that "No" is just not getting the point across all by itself.

Here is where the three-point teaching technique comes into play. We can go beyond just "no" and teach our children good coping mechanisms. They will not always take our suggestions but we can be confident that we gave them every possible way to avoid the consequence that comes with continuing an unwanted or harmful behavior (starting around 15-18 months).

o Step 1 – Identify the unwanted behavior.
o Step 2 –State the consequence.
o Step 3 –Teach the desired behavior.

Example:
o Step 1: "Sterling, do not throw that toy at your sister."
o Step 2: "If you do that again, you will go straight to "Simmer Time" (which is like "time-out" but different, we will explain shortly).
o Step 3: "What I want you to do is to play nicely with your sister. Get the puzzle out, you enjoy playing with that together."

Now, as a parent of a toddler, you know what will happen next. Often, Sterling does not take the alternate direction and she promptly throws a toy at her sister, again. We gave her a great chance to make a better choice and we are all on the same page. So, we do not need to threaten, cajole or ask useless questions. We simply follow the clearly stated course of action that we set forth and we PUT HER DIRECTLY IN SIMMER TIME.

What if she picks up the toy (that she just threw after you told her not to) and smiles at you as she prepares for another throw? Even though it is not exactly a 'throw' – it is a challenge. If she does not put it down immediately...PUT HER DIRECTLY IN SIMMER TIME.
What if she starts having a tantrum? PUT HER DIRECTLY IN SIMMER TIME.
What if she throws another toy and *then* says she is sorry and her little pouty face is bathed in cuteness? PUT HER DIRECTLY IN SIMMER TIME.
You see the end of this process is just as important as the beginning! Here is the full technique:

- o Step 1 – Identify the Unwanted Behavior.
- o Step 2 – State the Consequence.
- o Step 3 – Teach the Desired Behavior.
- o Most importantly, when they misbehave again, follow through with your discipline. It makes you trustworthy.
- o **Once you have followed through with the consequence: Always follow-up with a {HUG}**
  - **H - H**old them close,
  - **U - U**se confident face and
  - **G - G**ive positive feedback

We went forward with our consequence to get the opportunity to get her OUT of Simmer Time! That is when we have unprecedented access to her heart, and a powerful opportunity to tell her that we believe in her ability to do what we just asked her to do.

Once she has gone to Simmer Time and she settles down, we can do something incredibly necessary and valuable. We clearly state why she was there and how we believe in her ability to do the right thing in the future: "Sterling, you are here because you disobeyed Mommy and threw a toy at your sister." Then we let her know that we believe in her with the positive feedback: "But I know that you can listen to Mommy and I know that you will be great at treating your sister nicely. Let's go back out, say sorry to your sister and get that puzzle." (Resist the urge to put "OK?" at the end. You can replace it with "You will be great at that!")

See what an opportunity we just had to really place something valuable in her heart? By following this simple technique, we

1. Kept our frustration from escalating into anger.
2. Proved that we are reliable, confident and trustworthy.
3. Showed that forgiveness is always available in our household.
4. Helped our toddler recognize the importance of her behavior.
5. Allowed our toddler to take responsibility for her misbehavior.
6. Best of all, we were able to become her biggest supporter by telling her we believed in her ability to do what we asked her to do!

Most importantly, we allowed the consequence to help open her heart up so we could get that {**HUG**} moment, making that positive feedback even more important to her.

If we follow through with our stated disciplinary technique, at the end, we tell our child that we love them and we know that they are capable of being nice and obeying mommy and daddy.

This process reveals that we are trustworthy and that is a huge part of helping to meet their powerful desire for security. Another valuable lesson found in the {HUG} moment is that it conveys that forgiveness and restitution are always available in this household! They will know that no matter what happens, my mom and/or dad believes in me and will always be there for me.

If we ignore this process, then we miss out on innumerable opportunities to show that we are trustworthy and that forgiveness prevails in this house. Do not linger on the discipline itself—be confident that the process has a greater goal. It is an opportunity to shape our child's character and their understanding of the world around them.

Three-Point Teaching Technique Cheat Sheet

1. Identify the unwanted behavior
2. State the consequence
3. Teach the desired behavior
4. Once you have followed through with the consequence: Always follow-up with a {HUG}

   H - **H**old them close,
   U - **U**se confident face and
   G - **G**ive positive feedback

Simmer Time Guidelines

Ok, let's talk about that "Simmer Time" consequence.

Time Out vs. Simmer Time

For many parents, "time-out" is not working. Some of you have a little girl that would stand in "time-out" for a good 15 minutes playing "pretty-pretty princess" in her imaginary world and spinning in circles with her imaginary dress swirling in the wind, completely content.

So, in order to increase the effectiveness of our disciplinary technique, we have to disassemble a common myth - and that is the timetable that was placed on "time-out." One minute per year of age will not open your child's heart. They have to stay in a safe and separate environment until they stop crying or stay in there long enough that they begin to not like it. If we go in too soon, it will not work. One minute per year of age is simply not long enough.

If they are not fazed by "time-out" then they stay in a safe and separate environment (outlined below) until they are asking to come out or until a maximum time of 15-20 minutes has been reached. If they are in the midst of a full-blown tantrum, and we are nearing 15-20 minutes or the limit on your own inner clock (you get to choose), then we want to go and give them that hug and see if they will settle down so that we can have our teachable moment.

If we go in while our child is still crying and try to talk to them while they are crying, then our words are lost. Nothing gets through in the midst of a tantrum. That is not a teachable moment. Once they settle down, we can move forward. We have to wait for that moment—and it may take 5 minutes or 20—but we cannot be successful until they settle down and then that window opens and we have our opportunity to really make a difference. If you are just horrified by 20 minutes, then make it 5-10 minutes. Make it something that will work for you and will seem to be effective in your household.

Simmer Time is what time-out should really look like if it is to be effective, positive and helpful.

Placing a toddler in "Simmer Time" helps them to take responsibility for their actions. The best way for them to learn how to manage the frustration of a consequence is to allow them time to "simmer." Learning to manage their actions and frustrations takes time and opportunity. Using a "Simmer Time" helps them to learn how to settle down.

They can learn how to settle down even after getting to that intense crying tantrum state. We often say, "Oh, they get so worked up that they can't settle themselves down." What is the truth here? They most certainly CAN settle themselves down, but it takes TIME and they will never do it if they never have the opportunity.

We, as parents, do not enjoy the discipline part – actually having to put them in a safe but separate environment is not fun. It requires time and patience, which are in short supply. However, if we skip this part then we miss out on teaching our children this incredible concept which is crucial to their understanding of our character and theirs. So, let's transform the understanding of the process; making it accessible for the modern parent.

Simmer Time should be done in a place that is
- o Safe – meaning, completely child-proofed.
- o Has light and space.
- o It needs to be a place where they cannot see you. If you have ever watched a tantrum, you know that the show is just for you. They will kick and scream and then look up to make sure you are watching.
- o You can use a pack 'n play if your child does not know how to climb out. (A pack 'n play that is a different color then the one used for sleeping during vacation.)
- o We do not recommend the time-out chair because they know that you can see them there and will misbehave or try to engage you in conversation. Some may even taunt you from the time-out chair. If you have to hold them there or keep putting them back in the chair then it punishes you and does not give *you* time to settle down and determine how *you* are going to put a positive truth, a {HUG}, in your child's heart.
- o It lasts until they either calm down or until they are asking to come out. If they make it past your comfort level, then you can go in and soothe them but wait until they are finished crying before you have your {HUG} moment.
- o Only used for misbehaviors and tantrums, not for crying over an injury or a broken toy.
- o We do not have to catch every infraction. Use this as consistently as reality allows and with grace. We are doing this so we can get that {HUG} moment at the end.
- o You can use any child-proofed room with light and space. If you want to use your child's room then take two pieces of construction paper, one red and one

green. Place the paper securely, higher than 4 feet up and near the door so that you can turn it to the red side when they are in their room for Simmer Time and on the green side when they are in there for naps or playtime.

- On your way out of their room for Simmer Time – place it very purposefully on the red side. Do not look at them; do not explain it to them; do not do anything but place it on the red side and then get out fast.
- You may have to peel the child off of your leg to keep them in the room and get out as quickly as possible. And whatever you do, TRY NOT TO MAKE STRESS FACE. Do not let them see you sweat. This is an engagement-free zone until we come back for the **{HUG}** moment.
- When you do come back in, use the **{HUG}** moment. Their heart is now open for instruction. Keep it short, confident and to the point.
  - **H - H**old them close,
  - **U - U**se confident face and
  - **G - G**ive positive feedback. For example: "Hey, I know that you know how to obey Mommy. Now let's get out there, apologize to your sister and move on. You've got this."

Simmer Time for **Tantrums**

- **It is OK for a toddler to be frustrated but not OK for them to emotionally hijack the whole household.**
- At any time that your child begins to emotionally hijack the household with a screaming fit, they can go directly to Simmer Time.
- We do not use a three point teaching technique for tantrums.
- If we tell our child that they cannot have ice cream and they have a total break down over it, that indicates to us that they need to move to a place where they can settle down. So, directly to Simmer Time without any questions.
- Once they have settled down then we have a great chance to have our **{HUG}** moment. For example; we tell them that we know that they can live without ice cream for breakfast and that they will be great at listening to Mommy. Then we move on with our day.
- If tantrums work, they will be repeated.
- By using Simmer Time, we give our toddlers time and opportunity to practice managing their own frustrations. It places the responsibility for managing their frustrations where it belongs – with them.
- They just have to have a safe place to work out that normal human emotion of frustration every now and then.
- This also gives *us* a great opportunity to calm down and figure out what positive statement we want to make when their hearts are finally open to receive it, at the end of simmer time.

Simmer Time is a great place for them to simmer when they have misbehaved or when they have a tantrum. It helps them to learn to control their frustration and calm down. It is also an effective time for us to regroup, simmer down and plan our {HUG} moment.

Some children will take longer than others. Some will fall asleep in Simmer Time especially if it is close to naptime. If that happens, just save the {HUG} for when they awaken and then tell them how they can obey Mommy or treat the others with kindness.

Parents often think that the magic is in the disciplinary tool. But that is not the key. You see, life is not experienced in slices, it is experienced as a whole. If we can intervene incident by incident as much as is realistic AND we meet them between awake and asleep AND we use triangulation, then we are well on our way to having a satisfying and enjoyable parenting experience. The things that we want to establish more than anything else are families that are feeling more successful and have more time to enjoy each other.

When we use Simmer Time or any form of discipline, do not gauge success based on whether or not the child continues to misbehave. Toddlers misbehave; it is their way of testing their boundaries. You are successful if the child does not like the immediate consequences of their actions. That opens the opportunity to place important truths in their hearts. Wait for it. It really works.

Each child does not respond to the same form of discipline. The way to know if your child responds to your form of discipline is if they do not like it. It is OK to have two different children who respond to two different discipline techniques. Throw out the notion that the children all have to respond to the same discipline technique. It's also important to note that every discipline technique, if used to the extreme, can be harmful (i.e. misusing "time out" by putting a toddler in a dark closet).

In itself, the three point teaching technique is an effective tool, which can help parents to utilize any reasonable consequence of their choosing and manage their own frustrations more effectively. The three point teaching technique used with any consequence gives us a plan. When we do NOT have a plan, we are at a greater risk for reacting negatively.

There are multiple examples of creative tools that help with common toddler behavior issues in this book. Use what is helpful to you from this book and every other book. We also have a network of certified consultants available to work one-on-one with you and your family to help find the tools that will bring out the best behavior in your toddler.

Above all else, remember that you are the parent; you get to choose.

Messing Up – We All Do It

Now, because we are talking about reality, we must address this. We will fold. Sometimes in life, we will just give in. We do what it takes to keep things quiet. We ALL do it. So where do we go from there? What do we do when we have had a bad hair day, the dog had diarrhea all over the white carpet, the dishwasher repair man did not come in his committed "window of time" which made us late for our MOPS meeting and Alisa just called saying that she may have exposed our whole house to pink-eye yesterday?

What do we do when we give in? We carry on! We move forward! At naptime, we put ourselves in Simmer Time. We take time to get a breather, to stare at the wall and decompress. We treat ourselves with grace and regroup.

We earmark this page and tell ourselves that we can pull it together that we are the parent and our child is resilient. We concentrate on all the things we do right instead of this one little thing we think we did wrong.

We reassure ourselves that we HAVE NOT ruined everything. We may have some more testing of boundaries and tomorrow we may have to put our child in Simmer Time and that is OK. When we recommit, we will make progress.

Lay down the guilt, it is an unwanted bedfellow and it will steal your future confidence. Recognize that imperfect parents raise happy, healthy, well-adjusted children. It's going to be OK.

Say this to your own heart:
My child is resilient.
I am a good Mom/Dad/Caregiver and I can do this.

SUM IT UP

o The love that a parent has for their child is more powerful than the mistakes that they make.

o Remember, the goal is not perfection.

o You can do this.

NOTES

NOTES

ROUTINES AND SCHEDULES

Ecclesiastes 3:1
To everything there is a season, and a time to every purpose under heaven

Schedule

_____

_____

_____

Now we can cover a few other boundary stones that will help to set a good atmosphere in our households and help to meet our toddler's need for security

Boundary Stones

Obey Dad and Mom

Do not hurt others

Do not hurt yourself

Responsibilities

Faith

Schedule

Keys to Character Building

What if toddlers could make their own schedule each day? Would it look a bit like this?
- o Wake at 5 am
- o Jump in Mommy's bed (if not already there)
- o Color on baby brother's face with a sharpie marker while Mommy is in the shower
- o Cry until ice cream is served for breakfast
- o Throw ice cream on the floor
- o Terrorize cat

86

- Head outside in the cold in only light cotton pajamas, a tutu and a tiara while running out into the street chasing the dog, etc.

Toddlers thrive on a schedule; they just need someone smarter than them to decide what that should be. They are more apt to misbehave if they do not have some primary markers in their day. Primary markers are things that happen almost every day, something predictable in this unpredictable world.

We like to have about four primary markers in each day. We already have one covered, as the nighttime routine will be one primary marker that will stay the same, happen at the same time each night, with the same few steps every time. Another one can be a wake-up routine that begins with a big hug, then moves to the bathroom for potty time, washing hands and brushing teeth. If dad and/or mom is headed off to work and the family can meet together at the door to have a time of kisses and hugs, that will be a great way to promote family unity and a great primary marker for the day. Finally, the nap is an important primary marker.

Four primary markers:
- Wake-up routine.
- Meeting at the door to get hugs and kisses in the a.m. and/or dinner together later in the day.
- Naptime.
- Meeting between awake and asleep.

If you keep these things pretty consistent in your toddler's life, it will be another way to reinforce that their environment is secure and help them feel some sense that someone bigger than them has their life under control. Of course, like all things, we must balance this out. Some of us would like to schedule every minute of every day. However, we do want to provide some time for free play and occasional chaos is inevitable. Everything does not need to be structured, Harvard readiness training.

They are also born with a little inner 24-hour clock and when morning, naptime and bedtime happen at the same time each day, they feel very secure because it aligns with the way they are designed. They do not have to be able to tell time to respond to a schedule, it is built-in.

Another important thing to remember about schedules is that we can easily get overbooked with activities. We are looking for a good balance and that will be different in each household. A toddler, who does not have some down time in the day will be more prone to tantrums, act out more and occasionally be more aggressive. They cannot handle the hectic adult lifestyle. They need some unscheduled margin in life.

Toddler's lives often grow to mimic our own. So, we want to live our lives on purpose so that our children can grow up with a great sense of priorities. We have provided a worksheet that will help you to sort out the family priorities that are unique to your family. If you are a married couple, plan a date night and fill out your personal priorities and then combine them so you come up with the top five family priorities that feel right to you. You may want family time to be #1 or being connected to a church family or time for extended family or maybe it is important to have your children in organized sports or educational activities. Whatever is most important to you; list it every year.

Then use that list as a filter for other opportunities that come your way. If you are invited to 60 birthday parties during the course of the year and it is cutting into your time with extended family or having your children be a part of their grandmother's life, then graciously say, "I am sorry that we are unable to attend. We hope that it will be wonderful celebration. Thank you for the invitation."

It is OK to say no.

Having a family priority list will help you live your life in the way you intended and it will allow you to concentrate on the things that are truly important to you. It will also instill in your child a similar set of priorities that will help them to make decisions, as they get older, because they have seen it lived out in their loving home. They are likely to value the things that we value, so we need to be aware of the messages we are sending.

SUM IT UP

o   Determine your top 5 family priorities in order of importance
o   Take time to discuss them and write them down.
o   Give yourself permission to say "No" to even the 'good' things that do not promote your true family values or priorities.

Priorities Worksheet

_____

_____

_____

What things do you value? Put these in order of importance.

Mom Priorities
1.

2.

3.

4.

5.

Dad Priorities
1.

2.

3.

4.

5.

Meet together and meld those into your ...
Family Priorities
1.

2.

3.

4.

5.

90

Typical Days

How to use the typical days section:

The following schedules are guidelines. Any of the following schedules can be moved in their entirety ½ hour earlier or later to adjust to your personal home schedule.

We understand that schedules these days need to be flexible. We also know that the babies and toddlers who have regular nap times and feeding times tend to be more content. There is a delicate balance between being so scheduled that you cannot enjoy life and being so flexible that you cannot enjoy your family.

This is a gradual process and not black and white. We do not want to overwhelm you with details. If one schedule is working for you and you are not ready to progress to the next, then stay with that one as long as it is working.

When you see a "/" between two times listed in the schedules that means you can start anytime between those two times.

Morning naps should continue as long as you can possibly get them to take one! Usually, they will go down to one nap around 15 months. (See nap section for details.)

Note: DO NOT TAKE THE SIPPY CUP WITH MILK IN IT TO BED; IT CAN ERODE THEIR TEETH!

Typical Day 12-15 months

Two naps per day. Use this schedule until you drop the second nap.

7 a.m.	Door opens for start of day + sippy cup
7:30/8 a.m.	Breakfast: Protein, grain, fruit/veggie, whole milk
9:00 a.m.	Nap (ideally 1-1 ½ hours)
10/10:30 a.m.	Sippy cup + snack
12:00 p.m.	Lunch: Protein, grain, fruit/veggie, whole milk
12:30/1:30 p.m.	Nap: Pick one time between 12:30 and 1:30 and start nap at that time each day (ideally 1 ½ hours).
3:00 p.m.	Sippy cup + snack
5/6 p.m.	Family supper sometime between 5pm and 6pm.
6:30 p.m.	Bath
7/7:30 p.m.	Bedtime (See Sleep section.)

*Mealtimes include bite-sized, mushable versions of what you are having plus a sippy cup of whole milk. (Avoid low-fat milk for toddlers; they need healthy fats.)
 *Sippy cups have 2-6 ounces of whole milk and there are <u>no more bottles.</u>

Typical Day 12 months-4 years

One nap per day. Use this schedule once you drop the second nap (typically between 12 and 15 months).

7 a.m.	Door opens for start of day + sippy cup
8 a.m.	Breakfast: Protein, grain, fruit/veggie, whole milk
9:00 a.m.	Playtime (Work at keeping them awake.)
10 a.m.	Sippy cup + snack
11/11:30 a.m.	Lunch: Protein, grain, fruit/veggie, whole milk
12/1:00 p.m.	Nap: Pick one time between 12:00 and 1:00 and start nap at that time each day (ideally 2- 3 hours).
3:30/4 p.m.	Sippy cup + snack
5/6 p.m.	Family supper sometime between 5pm and 6pm.
6:30 p.m.	Bath
7/7:30 p.m.	Bedtime (See Sleep section.)

*Mealtimes include bite-sized, mushable versions of what you are having plus a sippy cup of whole milk. (Avoid low-fat milk for toddlers; they need healthy fats.)

Toddler + Newborn

The first few weeks of life for a family with a new baby is a beautiful but chaotic time. The baby will be feeding every 2-3 hours and their schedule takes precedence in the household. It is at this time that the toddler gets the opportunity to watch a family do the most amazing thing— work together to meet the needs of the youngest and weakest member.

This is a time when the toddler gets to assume additional responsibility and the first seeds of self-control begin to grow. The important thing to remember is to extend grace to the toddler, yourself and the whole household. At times, life with multiple children will seem difficult to manage and overwhelming, but at other times it will take your breath away with satisfaction and intense feelings of joy.

See the "Bringing Home Baby" Cheat sheet at the end of this resource for additional pointers. Get through each day the best that you can, knowing that your toddler will benefit from this experience; it will not ruin them.

The following schedule guidelines are for the multiple-child households starting with a baby who is healthy and gaining weight at 2 weeks of age. We wanted to give you an idea of what the day could look like. These schedules will provide a great starting point. You can adjust these schedules by a ½ hour in either direction to accommodate your household.

In the following schedules, we have taken great care to arrange for moms and dads to have:

o   Time to run errands

o A 1-2 hour break each day with both children napping!
o The maximum amount of nighttime sleep available (which can be 9-12 hours in a row starting at 3-4 months of age for breast and bottle fed babies that are using the Moms on Call baby guidelines).

For households with children of multiple ages, you can use the following schedules in accordance with this resource or see the Moms on Call Scheduler App for additional options. There is a routine that suits your household! In addition, all of the baby care guidelines in the *Moms on Call Basic Baby Care: 0-6 months* book to learn how to establish healthy sleep habits for the baby.

Toddler + Baby 2-4 weeks old

6/7:00 a.m.   *You can do the first feeding for baby anytime between 6 and 7am. Then put them right back down in the crib to sleep. Feed at 6am if the baby is awake but, if the baby is asleep, then you can feed as late as 7am. Keep the rest of the schedule intact.*

7/7:30 a.m.   Toddler comes out of their room for the day.

7:30 a.m.   Toddler breakfast (If baby is awake, then they can sit in the bouncy seat or swing as you get breakfast for the toddler.)

9:00 a.m.   Baby feeds at this time regardless of when the baby ate last.

9/9:30 a.m.   Toddler to class/playtime or snack at home.

10:00 a.m.   Baby naps (ideally 2 hours). This is a great time to let the baby sleep in the car seat and get some errands done.

12:00 p.m.   Baby feeds (If you need to leave to get the toddler from school, remember that the schedule can be adjusted by ½ hour in either direction in its entirety.)

12:30 p.m.   Toddler lunch

1:00 p.m.   Toddler in their room for a nap until 3:00/3:30 (cry, play or sleep).

Baby naps (ideally 2 hours)

3:00 p.m.	Baby feeds
3:30 p.m.	Toddler up from nap + snack
4:00 p.m.	Baby naps (ideally 1 ½ - 2 hours)
5:00 p.m.	Toddler supper or playtime (option 1)
6:00 p.m.	Baby "Supper Feed" then has fussy time
6:30 p.m.	Toddler supper or playtime (option 2)
7:00 p.m.	Baby catnap (30-60 minutes) Toddler bathtime
7:30 p.m.	Toddler's 15 minute bedtime routine
8:30 p.m.	Baby bathtime (even if we have to wake them up for it)
9:00 p.m.	Baby has the nighttime feeding, gets swaddled and put in the crib for nighttime sleep.
1am/5 a.m.	Baby may have nighttime feedings around 1 a.m. and 5 a.m. and then transition to 2 a.m. and 6 a.m. (according to the instructions found in the *Moms on Call Basic Baby Care: 0-6 months* book).

Toddler + Baby 1-3 months

6/7:00 a.m.	*You can do the first baby feeding anytime between 6 and 7am. Then put them right back down in the crib to sleep. Feed at 6am if the baby is awake but, if the baby is asleep, then you can feed as late as 7am. Keep the rest of the schedule intact.*
7/7:30 a.m.	Toddler comes out of their room for the day.
7:30 a.m.	Toddler breakfast (If baby is awake, then they can sit in the bouncy seat or swing as you get breakfast for the toddler.)
9:00 a.m.	Baby feeds at this time regardless of when the baby ate last.
9/9:30 a.m.	Toddler to class/playtime or snack at home.
10:00 a.m.	Baby naps (ideally 2 hours) This is a great time to let the baby sleep in the car seat as you run a few errands.
12:00 p.m.	Baby feeds (If you need to leave to get the toddler from school, remember that the schedule can be adjusted in its entirety by ½ hour in either direction.)
12:30 p.m.	Toddler lunch
1:00 p.m.	Toddler in their room for a nap until 3:00/3:30pm (cry, play or sleep). Baby naps (ideally 2 hours)

3:00 p.m.	Baby feeds
3:30 p.m.	Toddler up from nap + snack
4:00 p.m.	Baby naps (ideally 1-1 ½ hours)
5:00 p.m.	Toddler supper or playtime (option 1)
5:30 p.m.	Baby "Supper Feed" then has fussy time
6:30 p.m.	Toddler supper or playtime (option 2)
7:00 p.m.	Baby catnap (30-60 minutes) Toddler bathtime
7:30 p.m.	Toddler's 15 minute bedtime routine
8:00 p.m.	Baby bathtime (even if we have to wake them up for it)
8:30 p.m.	Baby has the nighttime feeding, gets swaddled and put in the crib for nighttime sleep
2/3 a.m.	Baby may have nighttime feeding (according to the instructions found in the *Moms on Call Basic Baby Care: 0-6 months* book).

Alternate Option
Toddler + Baby 6 weeks - 4 months

7:00 a.m.	Baby BF/bottle then awake and playful
7:30 a.m.	Toddler comes out of room for the day.
8:00 a.m.	Toddler breakfast
8:30 a.m.	Baby naps (ideally 1-1 ½ hours)
9/9:30 a.m.	Toddler to class/playtime or snack at home. From 9-10am is the best time to get errands done.
10:00 a.m.	Baby BF/bottle
11:00 a.m.	Baby naps
12:00 p.m.	Toddler lunch
1/1:30 p.m.	Baby BF/bottle
	Toddler in their room for a nap until 3:00/3:30pm (cry, play or sleep).
2:00 p.m.	Baby naps (ideally 1 ½-2 hours; this is where you can have an hour to yourself.)
3:30/4 p.m.	Toddler up from nap + snack
4:00 p.m.	Baby up from nap + BF/bottle
5:30/6 p.m.	Baby optional catnap

6:00 p.m.	Family supper (Just let baby sit with you or in the bouncy seat and get a feel for what family mealtime looks like.)
6:30 p.m.	Baby bath (Bottle feeding moms, get the baby's bottle ready ahead of time for a feeding after the bath.)
7:00 p.m.	Last nighttime feeding for baby. Put baby in crib, white noise on, close the door.
7:30 p.m.	Toddler bath
7:50 p.m.	Toddler nighttime routine and door closed by 8:15pm

(Baby nighttime feedings can be stretched according to the instructions found in the *Moms on Call Basic Baby Care: 0-6 months* book.)

Toddler + Baby 4-6 months
(after starting baby foods)

7:00 a.m.   Baby BF/bottle then awake and playful

7:30 a.m.   Toddler comes out of room for the day.

8:00 a.m.   Toddler and baby breakfast

9:00 a.m.   Baby naps (ideally 1-1 ½ hours)

9/9:30 a.m.   Toddler to class/playtime or snack at home. From 9-10am is the best time to get errands done.

11:00 a.m.   Baby BF/bottle

12:00 p.m.   Toddler and baby lunch

1:00 p.m.   Toddler in their room for a nap until 3:00/3:30pm (cry, play or sleep).

Baby naps (ideally 1 ½-2 hours; this is where you can have an hour to yourself.)

3:00 p.m.   Baby up from nap + BF/bottle

3:30 p.m.   Toddler up from nap + snack

4:00 p.m.   Baby supper (baby food)

5:30/6 p.m.   Baby optional catnap (Although it is more likely family playtime – get out energy!)

6/6:30 p.m.	Family supper and baby has a baby food snack (Just let baby sit with you and get a feel for what family mealtime looks like.)
6:50 p.m.	Bottle feeding moms, get the baby's bottle ready for after the bath and place it in the toddler's room on a dresser.
7:00 p.m.	Toddler bath/baby bath (If the baby is not yet sitting up without support, then the baby can be in the *bathroom (not in the bath)* in a bouncy seat for all the action and the kids are bathed one after the other. QUICK! Bathing at the same time starts around 5-6 months when the baby can sit up in a bath chair.)
7/7:30 p.m.	Get both kids dressed and either "divide and conquer" (one parent per child) or feed the baby while doing the Toddler's nighttime routine. Have the Toddler come with you as you place the baby in the crib for nighttime sleep and then finish the Toddler's bedtime routine, starting with the Household Rules.

No more middle of the night feedings! Everyone is resting in their own rooms, all night (except when they are sick).

Toddler + Baby 7-12 months

7:00 a.m.   Baby BF/bottle then awake and playful

7:30 a.m.   Toddler comes out of room for the day.

8:00 a.m.   Toddler and baby breakfast (Baby has a sippy cup with 2-4 ounces of formula or breastmilk.)

9:00 a.m.   Baby naps (ideally 1-1 ½ hours)

9/9:30 a.m.   Toddler to class/playtime or snack at home. This is the perfect time to run errands.

10:30/11 a.m.   Baby up from nap + BF/bottle.

12/12:30 p.m.   Toddler and baby lunch (Baby has a sippy cup with 2-4 ounces of formula or breastmilk.)

1:00 p.m.   Toddler in their room for a nap until 3:00/3:30pm (cry, play or sleep).

                 Baby naps (ideally 1 ½-2 hours; this is where you can have at least an hour to yourself.)

3:00 p.m.   Baby up from nap + BF/bottle. As baby gets older, baby has finger food snack and, if did not take from the sippy cup well, can BF/give bottle here.

3:30 p.m.   Toddler up from nap + snack
104

5:00 p.m.	Baby supper (baby foods + sippy cup)
5:30/6 p.m.	Family playtime – get out energy!
6/6:30 p.m.	Family supper and baby has a baby finger food snack (Just let baby sit with you and get a feel for what family mealtime looks like. At about 10-11 months of age, this becomes the baby's supper feeding instead of the 5pm supper.)
6:50 p.m.	Bottle feeding moms, get the baby's bottle ready for after the bath and place it in the toddler's room on a dresser.
7:00 p.m.	Toddler bath/baby bath together
7:30 p.m.	Get both kids dressed and either "divide and conquer" (one parent per child) or feed the baby while doing the Toddler's nighttime routine. Have the Toddler come with you as you place the baby in the crib for nighttime sleep and then finish the Toddler's bedtime routine.

NOTES

NOTES

_____

_____

_____

RESPONSIBILTY AND MORAL VALUES

Micah 6:8
He has showed you, O man, what is good; and what does the LORD require of you, but to do justly, and to love mercy, and to walk humbly with your God?

Responsibility

Raising toddlers is a messy business. You may be looking at your once white carpet and wondering if they make a steam cleaner that follows you through the house each day. That white couch you brought into the marriage that was once the pinnacle of home décor is now sporting vibrant pillows to cover the stains from that runaway cupcake and a discoloration from last year's stomach virus. The great news is that it does get better. And we do not always have to wait.

Toddlers can pick up their own toys, put a paper plate in the trash, bring their utensils to the sink after a meal, dust, wipe counters, sweep with a small sweeper and clean up spills. It is time consuming and it will not be done to perfection but they can do it and the more fun we make it, the more they will pitch in. We cannot expect toddlers to live a mess-free life but just like with the schedule we can find a happy balance that works.

When you have a multiple child household, sometimes you have to let go of the unrealistic view of the perfect household. **When you have multiple children, you will not be perfect parents with perfect robot toddlers living a quiet, mess-free existence**. We can learn to embrace the unexpected messes of life and when we do, we become less uptight. So let us give you permission today to have a messy house sometimes. It will make you a better parent.

However, it is important for toddlers to have the opportunity to contribute to the household. Remember that toddlers can follow a two-part command, such as "Pick up your paper plate AND throw it in the trash." If you give too many steps, they get overwhelmed and will not participate.

Let's use our excellent communication skills and allow them to help us. It will develop a useful life skill.
"Now it is time to play clean up. Let's see how fast we can get these toys in the basket...ready set go! 1...2...3...4...5......" or "Time to sing the clean up song."
"Time to sweep the floor. You are mommy's great helper. I love the way that you hold the dustpan for me. Get the dustpan and hold it right here"
"Ut-oh a spill! You know who is great at cleaning spills? That's right you are! Here is a napkin, take it to the spill and rub up all the apple juice. You are doing a great job!"

Help them and assist as needed. If they say "no", you say: "Not 'No', 'Yes ma'am' and do it. I will help you." Then help them to do it. Keep it really positive. Sometimes they are just not interested or you do not have the strength or clarity of thought to help them through the process. That is reality so do this as often as you can.

SUM IT UP

o Over the next week, find two or three ways that your child can contribute to the household.
o Patiently give them 1-2 sentence instructions.
o Say to yourself "My house may be dirty today but my children are loved and it's going to be OK."

Faith

It is important to connect our children with moral values and directions beyond ourselves. The faith boundary stone is the capstone. Children have a sense of belonging and family unity when they are included in the family's faith traditions. It is a way to connect our children to something bigger than we are and something that will speak into their lives when we are not around. Oftentimes, your faith determines your priorities. Listen to these words from an ancient proverb from King Solomon, "Raise a child in the way he should go and when he is old, he will not depart from it."

At the very least determine to find people who have similar values and set aside time to be together with them. We want to institute every layer of protection in our power for our toddlers. This does not mean that we have to shield them from differing belief systems, it just means that we give them a sense of belonging to a group that shares our moral values beyond just our family.

Toddlers are not in the business of picking out their own religion, they want the security of knowing that they belong to something real and good and dependable and bigger than they are. For Laura and I, that means connecting them to our Savior, Jesus Christ.

We do want to let it be known that when we set out to design these materials, we purposefully designed them for every parent that was struggling and needed some basic direction. You may have noticed that these resources can help people of any faith. It has always been the goal of Moms on Call to reach out to all who are in need. Our clients have been from all walks of life and many faiths and it has been our honor to serve you all in the best way we can.

SUM IT UP

- o   If you have not yet discussed how you are going to set up the spiritual foundation of your household, discuss it with your spouse or the other primary influencers in your child's life.
- o   Research what is available in your community to help support you in the decisions that you have made for your home.

SLEEPING ALL NIGHT AND HAVING FUN AT MEALTIME

Proverbs 3:24
When you lie down, you will not be afraid; Yes, you will lie down and your sleep will be sweet.
Luke 12:29
And do not set your heart on what you will eat or drink; do not worry about it.

Sleeping All Night

Now, let us cover the two boundary stones that keep us the busiest: sleeping and feeding. These two can make or break a household.

Keys to Character Building

Of all of the helpful ways that we have successfully reduced stress, sleep is the most appreciated.

If your toddler is sleeping in your bed and kicking you in the ribs all night long or taking up ¾ of a king-sized bed where you wake up clinging for your life on the last available 2 inches of the mattress, you are not alone. Or maybe, you are curled into a little fetal position with cold feet sticking out from beneath a blanket on a toddler bed.

If your household is being run by a toddler as soon as bedtime is mentioned, you may be reading this book desperate, sleep-deprived and at the end of your rope. Perhaps your evening is dedicated to getting special blankets, cups of water, endless trips to the potty or putting a child back in their room for the tenth time. Or it could be that you are just about to transfer to that toddler bed and are scared about how your toddler will handle that transition.

Whatever your current sleep situation, if you feel it is unsustainable or filled with stress, we need to reevaluate and make changes where they are needed in positive and helpful ways. We will give you a specific plan.

How does this sound? A nice relaxing and fun nighttime routine that ends with everyone sleeping in their own room and in their own bed ALL NIGHT LONG— including you! That is where we are headed and getting there is a mess, but we will march through the difficult moments with that goal in mind. Healthy sleep habits lead to content children and happy families.

Let's establish that you love your child and will be reinforcing your child with positive statements BEFORE bed such as:
- o "You can do this."
- o "I believe in you."
- o "You are so brave."
- o "I love you"

All of the sleep instructions have a goal in mind. To transform stressful, sleep deprived families that are hanging on for dear life into well-rested confident families who can revel in the sheer delight of family life. We want you to be clear-minded while you are doing the fun stuff and avoid being tired, curt or irritated as much as possible.

The number one thing we have to establish before we get started is that your toddler is capable of self-control and capable of getting themselves to sleep and staying asleep. We believe that they can do it and back our words up with actions. If we tell them we believe that they can get to sleep but then come back into the room five times or give up/sleep in their room, then we are not sending consistent messages.

If you want your child to learn to fall asleep in their own room and stay asleep in their room, you will need to cling to the fact that your child is fully capable of doing this. And we also have to know how long it will take for them to learn it. It does not take 10 minutes, an hour or even one night. It typically takes about 3-5 days for a toddler transferring to a toddler bed for the first time and up to 2 full weeks for stubborn toddlers who have previously developed some unsustainable habits.

No matter how long it takes, the process is no fun. The transition is hard but great things will happen along the way and your child will know that you believe in them, even when they do not yet believe in themselves. That is something that we as parents want to be doing for our children throughout their entire lives.

We cannot learn to sleep FOR them. We support them with the truth and the most ideal sleep environment (one that lacks the stimulation of say, well, us) and then we allow *them* to learn how to sleep.

Send consistent messages so your children know beyond a shadow of a doubt that you believe in them and before you
118

know it, they are believing in themselves. This requires us to use everything we learned in this resource and then back it all up with ACTION.

There are other methods out there and as the parent, you get to choose what you feel will work best for your family. If you decide to use this method, before you start, you have to be absolutely committed.

This method is intent on encouraging you to support your toddler, which will ultimately help them to adjust to healthy nighttime habits.

They need long stretches of sleep just like we do. Give it one or two weeks and you can look forward to evening time, decrease the unhealthy levels of stress in the household each night, get full night's of restful sleep and maybe even have a chance to have time in the evening with your spouse to remember why you made babies. But the most important thing of all is that you communicated to your toddler that they could do this, backed that up with action and when they do sleep all night in that room you decorated just for them, the sense of achievement for that toddler is astounding. You gave them something valuable. You gave them confidence that they could do it. Now, let's get started with a few ground rules:

Basics
- Toddlers need about 14 hours of sleep per day. 10-12 of those should be "in a row" at nighttime.
- Control over bladder and bowel habits does not kick in until between 3 to 5 years of age. So, pull-ups/diapers are for nighttime until your child has one full week of staying dry at night. We are not potty training at nighttime or naptime.

o If we are just transferring to a toddler bed, we put all the guidelines in place so that they never know that mommy sleeping in their toddler bed or 2 hours of asking for water is even an option.
o We move to a toddler bed when (whichever comes first):
    o They can climb out of the crib.
    o We need the crib for baby #2.
    o You just want to move them and they seem ready.
    o They reach their third birthday.
    o See Cheat Sheet at the back of this resource entitled "Transferring to a Toddler Bed".
o Do not take a sippy cup of milk to bed, it can erode a toddler's teeth.
o We do not sleep train when our child is legitimately sick. If it happens in the middle of sleep training, then we stop and restart once they are feeling better.

Middle of the night feedings
o It's time to get off the 24-hour digestion train. There should not be any reason to feed a healthy toddler in the middle of the night. They will not starve because they miss a feeding at 2 a.m.
o Digestion is too stimulating for nighttime.

Sleep Environment
o **Adult white noise machines** are an essential piece of the puzzle. They need to be loud enough for you to hear them from outside the toddler's room with the door closed. We have a link to the one we like best at www.momsoncall.com. This noise helps to lull the brain into that restorative and restful REM sleep that

is so essential to growth and development. White noise only (Don't play nature sounds).
- o **A night-light,** is optional. We recommend The Good Nite Lite (goodnitelite.com). You can set the "sun to come up" at any specific morning time that suits your family schedule within reason.
- o **A <u>visual monitor</u>** as an added safety feature is fine as long as you are not glued to it for hours. If they know you can see them, they will put on a show for you, keep that in mind. Do not engage them through this device – or at all. They are very smart.
- o The ideal temperature of the room is 68-72 degrees.

Safety
- o The child's room is childproofed—completely. Here are some things to look out for, but this is not an exhaustive list. **This step is crucial.**
- o Outlets are covered (you can get outlet covers for plugged in items at hardware stores)
- o All tall dressers or shelves are anchored to the wall so they cannot tip over.
- o There are no heavy objects like televisions on top of dressers that could fall on top of a child.
- o The blind cords are cut so nothing is dangling and posing a strangulation hazard.
- o All items that can be ingested, such as medication, diaper cream and shampoo, are locked away and not just in a drawer in their room.
- o If there is a door in their room that leads to a bathroom, it is closed and locked restricting any access that a toddler has to a bathroom with running water or other dangers. If that is the only way into the bathroom then install an eye/hook latch at the top of the door to keep it secure.

- o **Turn the doorknob around on their door so it locks from the outside/hallway side** —this is crucial. Just like the crib-restricted access to the room, the closed/locked door restricts access to the dangers in the house.

How Daytime affects Night time sleep
- o We are setting their little inner 24-hour clock.
- o Start the day on time. There is no "making up" for lost sleep. Try to keep the routine intact as much as reality allows.
- o See the "Typical Days" section for sample daily routines.
- o Because the demands of households with multiple children can vary, there are 2 options: the MOC scheduler App which contains side-by-side schedules and this resource which has combined schedule options. Choose which suits your household. They all work.
- o Naptime should be over by 4 p.m. If the naps are too long or go too late they can affect nighttime sleep.
  - o If your toddler is taking two naps a day then neither lasts over two hours.
  - o If they are going to one nap a day then that nap can last up to 3 hours

Bedtime routine
- o If just transferring to a toddler bed, then we start this the day the new bed is ready and set up in their room.
- o Start with a bath, every night.
- o Then we go in their room and get them in their jammies and dance, play or have those **uninterrupted moments of sheer enjoyment that we call "tender time."** Then we start the nighttime routine. (Once they go in their room after bath time,

they stay in their room.)
- Read no more than 2 books.
- Go over the household rules
- One thing they did great
- One thing we are working on together
- Then, "Tonight you are going to get to sleep in your own room and sleep right here in your big kid bed. You are going to be so great at it! So here is how you start: pull up your bed covers, close your eyes and fall asleep. I am going to close the door to keep you safe. I love you, I believe in you and I will see you in the sun comes up."
- Then, white noise goes on, the main light goes off and the door closes and our "no engagement" policy begins.
- The door opens again in the morning regardless of pleas of any type, manipulative statements or crying. This way, you said that you believed in them and you put action behind your words.
- Do not go in the room and intervene unless you need to save them from getting hurt.

Before you make it out the door
- **What if they say they are scared of the door being closed?** Lovingly tell them that we do this to keep them safe and GET OUT AND CLOSE THE DOOR.
- **What if they say they are afraid of monsters**? They just need reassurance that they are safe. They need it in simple terms and may need to hear the same simple phrase night after night, but it will speak to the heart of the matter in a way that they can understand. We simply and confidently say, "You are safe and we love you" THEN GET OUT AND CLOSE THE DOOR.
- Have to go potty? If your child is not staying dry

through the night then "Nighttime is for pull-ups/diapers" THEN GET OUT AND CLOSE THE DOOR. Even potty trained children WILL use having to go to the potty as an excuse to get you back in the room. If your child stays dry at night, then we do not need to institute a nighttime pull-up or diaper. Limiting fluid intake after 6 pm can also be helpful in establishing dry mornings.

After you close the door

- o If they...get out of bed, bang on the door, say they have to go potty, need a drink, extra kisses, need my mommy, need one more book, need new pajamas, want to have a snack, want to tell you something.....
- o We will have a strict "**No engagement policy**" after that door closes. Your only job is NOT to go in that room or say anything through the door. We are not doing three point teaching techniques or going in to talk to them or "help them settle down." They *can* and *will* do that on their own with time and opportunity.

Why lock the door?

- o This is simply a safety measure so that the toddler does not have access to an entire house filled with dangers in the middle of the night when parents are sleeping. And we know that you are saying, "But they always just come to our room" or " they never go downstairs," but that is NOT a guarantee. It is too dangerous.
- o If there is a fire, an adult or firefighter will have to get them out of the house and they like to hide when they are scared, so we don't want to have to search a 3,000 square foot home, we want to be able to find them in a 10X10 foot room and know exactly where they are. We NEVER mention that scenario to our toddlers. We

simply tell them that we close the door to keep them safe.

- This is also important so that we can help them learn that their room is a safe and appropriate place for sleeping all night.
- For those of you who have just been waiting for permission to close that door, you have it. Close it and lock it from the hallway side to keep that child safe. They will be fine with it if *we* are fine with it.
- Our job is to stay out and **not to engage in any conversation**. We will not be addressing any behaviors, commenting on any requests or going back in the room, lest we fear for their lives. That is our entire job at night. It is the hardest thing you have ever had to do thus far. But we will tell our hearts the truth. The truth is:

THEY ARE SAFE.
THEY ARE LOVED.
THEY CAN LEARN TO DO THIS.

Special concerns

- **Throw toys at the door?** – Stay out. Address it in the morning. "You did not have to throw these toys all over when you'd be great at sleeping in your bed."
- **Hold onto you so you cannot leave?** Give them a substitute, and right before you head out the door, say "I love you, I believe in you and I will see you when the sun comes up," you make a big deal out of a special stuffed animal that you bought for them and tell them to show you how to hug it. Tell them to hug on the bear every time they need a hug and that it is a special bear that is just there for nighttime hugs to help kids fall fast asleep. Do not use a stuffed animal for toddlers under the age of 2 years.

- Pitch an all out tantrum when you close the door? Do it anyway, we ignore tantrums and their room should be child proofed so that they are safe. If it does not get you back in the room for a night or two, it will stop because they will learn that it does not work.
- **You are afraid that they will feel abandoned?** We parent by the truth. Are they abandoned? Are you taking off to Mexico to never see them again? NO, you are not. So, we will parent out of truth and not out of fear. They are not abandoned—period. You will show up every morning just like you said you would.
- **You are afraid they will wake up a sibling?** We never "save" the quiet one. Siblings have an innate ability to sleep through loudness. But if another child wakes, they can get themselves back to sleep without our help and will do so better without us in the room offering up extra stimulation in the middle of the night. We just let them work it out. First they learn how to accommodate their siblings then they learn how to accommodate classmates, then others in the community and so on. It is a natural part of life. Remember; we are not in the business of conflict avoidance but life-preparedness. We want to equip them to live in a household with brothers and/or sisters who may make noise sometimes at night.
- Any behavior that gets you back in the room will be repeated over and over, that is how we got here in the first place. Send them consistent messages. You know they can do it, *show* them that you believe in them by staying out of the way and letting them achieve all night sleep in their room.

We all need support
- During this process, we like to give Dads a little help too. So, their job is to roll over in the night, put their

arms around you and say, "We will get through this together." That is so much better than just rolling over and grunting, "They'll be fine, go back to sleep." But sometimes they need very specific instructions on how to support us in the way that our hearts will receive.

o Now, for dads who are having a hard time – Moms can roll over and say "We will get through this together" It works either way.
o Only proceed if you are both on the same page.

More helpful tips

1. We start the day at the same time each day. Typically between 7 and 8 am. We do not allow them to sleep in and "make up" for lost sleep but we transfer that lost sleep to the following night. Also, do not let them take extra naps or extra-long naps. We are setting up a healthy 24-hour day. We are setting that little internal clock to sleep at the same times each day and night.

2. Handle misbehaviors from the night before in the morning.
Anything that went on in that room the night before meets our completely unconcerned confident face and we make a clear statement and move on. There will be no three point teaching techniques and no freaking out over what happened. We will not let on that anything that went on the night before bothered us or shook our resolve. They can do this, that is our motto and we will stick to it with unwavering, unshakeable confidence. And you just watch because that confidence will be contagious.

We have an opportunity to put everything together that we

learned in this resource. We speak with clear direction, keep it short and we have our "confident face" on and that is when we address any antics that went on the night before such as ...

- o "You did not need to sleep here in front of the door when you could have slept in that comfy bed all night. Oh, well, you'll get the hang of it. Let's start our day."
- o "You didn't have to pull all your clothes out of your drawers last night when you'd be great at snuggling up in your bed and sleeping there all night. Oh, well, we'll get these picked up and start our day." – smile and confidence
- o "You didn't have to throw your pull-up in the corner. It stays on all night. Oh, well we'll throw this one out and you can have a fresh one at naptime. Let's start our day."
- o We do NOT ask them "Why" they did any of those things. We do NOT make stress face and we do not ask them if they were "scared". We simply communicate that this is a normal part of life that they will figure out.

3. If at first you don't succeed... This process takes up to two weeks for our stubborn ones if we stay out of the way. If we go in, and some of us might, then it takes longer but it can still be done. There is no point of no return. Regroup, reread the sleep section of the book and start fresh the next night. You can do it!! Let the toddler sleep in the lovely room that you decorated and prepared just for them. Let them figure it out. They can do it.

4. **Once a great nighttime is established we can have occasional late nights**. It is fine to have date night, a later family night on a weekend or a babysitter that does not

follow the routine exactly as you do. We are trying to establish a great foundation so that we can occasionally enjoy a deviation from the schedule.

What to Expect – Night by Night

Night One

- o You get out of the door and close it.
- o This night can be filled with pleas of various sorts, typically whatever has worked in the past (have to potty, need a drink, need Mommy, one more kiss/story/hug). Stay out and do not engage them through the door.
- o The first few hours can turn into a complete meltdown with kicking and yelling. Do not engage them; do not go in.
- o This talking/crying can seem like it carries on for most of the night on and off.
- o Start the morning at the same time. (7 am is what we recommend.) Do not let them "sleep in."
- o The hardest part of *day* one is keeping them awake at the right times. Naptimes are on schedule and do not last beyond 4 p.m. or go longer than usual.
- o The next night starts on time. Do not put them to bed earlier than the normal scheduled time (see Typical days).

Night Two

- o They are a bit more tired this night, which is helpful.
- o They will often try to "hold onto you" as you exit. Keep confident face. Get out and close the door.
- o There may be more pleading and crying like night one but not quite as long because they are more tired.
- o They may wake a couple times in the night and call for you. Do not engage and stay out. Even if they are

having another night of mostly crying.
- o In the morning, start the day on time and address any unwanted behaviors with a matter-of-fact tone. "You did not have to sleep in front of this door when you could have slept in your comfy bed all night and been great at it." Then start the day.
- o Keep them awake until the scheduled naptimes.

Night Three

- o Much like night two. They may plead with you before you get out the door with, "Why can't you stay in here with me?" or "I don't like the door shut." To which you confidently reply. 'We shut the door to keep you safe and you are going to be great at this". Discussion is over, and we say "I love you, I believe in you and I will see you when the sun comes up" and get out and close the door.
- o On and off wakings and some crying throughout the night
- o Start the day on time.
- o If they start to get very clingy when the bathtime starts, this is a very normal part of the process. You are not ruining them. You are believing in them. Your consistency and confidence will become contagious. It just takes time and opportunity. Keep "confident face." The message that your toddler receives is that they are going to be just fine and that this is simply a normal transition. Say that they can do this, simply over and over—do not try to reason with your toddler, just be repetitive and confident. "You are going to be just fine. You can do this."
- o You set the atmosphere in that bathroom and bedroom before bed. You stand on the truth with everything you've got. The truth is that they are safe, they are loved and they can learn to do this. Toddlers

131

will test you to see if you really believe this. It is a change for them so they get clingy as we transition them to all night sleep. But they will adjust to the new routine and love its consistency if we stay strong and confident.

- o Now, they may always want you to stay in their room longer, they typically do. But it will turn into just a request right before bed and then they settle into that wonderful dependable nighttime structure.
- o If you were just transferring to a toddler bed for the first time, then this may be the end of the hard part. Nighttime routines are established.

Nights 4-10

- o Much like night 3 but we may have a breakthrough night where they get right to sleep and stay asleep. This can be erratic for a few days as the healthy and consistent sleep habits sink in. It may be good sleep one night, bad the next.
- o Many of our clients begin to hear phrases like "Blakely did night-night!" and "Mary (referring to herself) is a good sleeper Mommy!" Some even tell their teacher at school, with confident enthusiasm "we close the door at night to keep me safe".

Nights 10-14

- o Now we are beginning to see a more consistent pattern of healthy sleep behaviors. The toddlers are depending more on the routine and less on your presence to get to sleep. They are doing it and they feel that sense of accomplishment. They still may not want you to leave the room and that is fine as long as you do not linger. Just repeat that, "I love you, believe in you and will see you when the sun comes up." Pretty soon they will be charming your friends and family with stories of achievement. "I am great at sleeping all night in my room." And it will be the truth!

When Good Sleep Patterns Get Interrupted

Your child's sleep pattern may be interrupted when:

o They reach certain developmental milestones - i.e., crawling, walking, speaking.
o They change environments or daily routines (vacation, holidays).
o They are recovering from an illness.
o We get rid of the paci.

This is where the sleep cycle can meet its doom. The good news is that if you will stay committed, they will get back to a well-established nighttime routine in a few nights. The longer you wait, the longer it will take them to revert back to the great routine that was in place. So, this means they will fuss and cry and what they really want is for you to enforce the boundary that was so solid at bedtime until they can get used to it again. It gets better with each subsequent night and with each transition.

Naptime

Toddlers will typically go to one naptime around 12-15 months. When they are ready to go to one naptime, it is the afternoon nap that will remain. Try not to start it later than 2pm. If they go to a school program and take a nap at noon then on the days they are home, start their nap at noon. If they do not have a designated naptime at school and get home after lunch then start the nap each day at the same time after lunch. If they have a baby sibling, then see the "typical days" section of this book for ideal schedules.

Toddlers need about 14 hours of sleep per day, so if they are sleeping 12 hours at night then they still need about a 2 hour nap each afternoon. If they resist naptime, keep it at the same time each day and for the same amount of time. **They can cry, play or sleep,** but they have that time set aside where they are not stimulated for the 2 hours in the afternoon. Typically, if you will keep the time the same each day and do not intervene and let them work it out, they will eventually get to sleep on their own. The maximum time for them to sleep in the afternoon is 3 ½ hours. If we go much longer than that, then it interrupts nighttime sleep. The afternoon nap should be over by 4:00 p.m. at the absolute latest.

Also, when they meet certain developmental milestones, their brain "wakes up" in certain areas and it makes it hard to sleep. They may have a 1-2 week period of interrupted naptime when they reach big developmental milestones and keeping the daily routine intact will help them to settle back into the normal patterns of life.

Our job is not to "make" our toddlers sleep. Which is good because we cannot "make" them sleep. Our job is to provide a consistent environment, opportunity and time for sleep. Every toddler should have a nap "opportunity" each day. They can cry, play or sleep. It is up to them but they stay in their room for the designated amount of time. This also makes the closed door with a lock on the outside a great tool. It helps them to recognize that they have a downtime each day, even on the days they do not want it.

If you want to occasionally nap with them then go right ahead. However, some toddlers will want you to be there every nap and can become dependent on that very easily, others will sleep if you are there or not. You know your child and whether they can handle it.

They can sleep as much as they want in the predetermined window but when the naptime is over, we get them up. The important thing that will help to decrease naptime frustration is to recognize that they will have their good nap days and their bad ones. Do not put them to bed early (at nighttime) on the bad nap days or else we throw off their 24-hour clock. Be consistent with the times that things happen to the best of your ability each day.

The primary concept that helps to reduce tension in the household and in our hearts is knowing what things are our responsibility. We can clearly tell our child when naptime begins, we can turn on the white noise, make it nice and cool in the room and give them kisses. Then we can close the door and open it 1 ½ to 3 hours later. But we cannot make them sleep. That is their job.

When Laura moved her 2-year-old into his new room, he did not want to take a nap. She put him in the childproofed room and closed the door and allowed him to cry. The first day took about 20 minutes of crying (which seems like forever at the time!), the second about 10 minutes, and by the third naptime he fussed about 2-3 minutes and was off to sleep. Did this break Laura's heart? Yes. Was this the best thing for Brent so he could learn to soothe himself to sleep? Definitely.

Now, let's look at a different scenario. If Laura had allowed Brent to come out of the room, he would have put on this crying episode every nap in order to be able to do something more fun. He also would have been incredibly tired and cranky for the rest of the night, which would be particularly unfortunate as Laura has four other children to manage. If Laura had given in and gone in the room to stay with Brent until he fell asleep, she just taught him how to be dependent on her presence in order to fall asleep. This will also affect nighttime sleeping. Teaching our children to get to sleep on their own will benefit the whole family.

Dropping the Morning Nap

12-15 months

These guidelines are for early toddlers that are getting 10-12 hours of nighttime sleep in a row. (If they are not, then read the nighttime sleep section and do that first)

- We will go to one nap typically between 12-15 months.
- We go to one nap when the child is having more bad nap days than good ones for 2 weeks given that you are using the other Moms on Call guidelines.
- Typically, the afternoon nap gets really unpredictable.
- The adjustment to one nap will take a week.
- Pick a start time between 12-1:30 p.m. Whatever time you choose is the time that the nap starts every day.
- The one nap is a minimum of 1 ½ hours long and a maximum of 3 hours long (from the start of the naptime, not the start of the time that they fell asleep).
- It needs to be over by 4pm.
- We will not ruin everything by having a weekend getaway or staying at the zoo too long; as long as we keep the same nap schedule in place when reality allows.
- When we are home, the nap can start at 12:30pm and that is how it will happen every day that we are at home.
- If we are doing so much running around each day that we cannot establish a regular naptime, they will

be cranky and will have a harder time adjusting to the daily routines. It does not make you a bad mom, it is a trade-off. In reality, some of us have unpredictable schedules for various reasons.

- o Naptimes are more successful when nighttime sleep of 10-12 hours in a row is firmly established.
- o The hardest part of the transition is keeping them awake until that one naptime for the first week.

To keep them awake, change environments, pat their heads with a cold washcloth and work at it. Avoid putting them in front of the TV/iPad at this time. There is also a cheat sheet in the back of this book for Naptime!

There are things we can control and things we cannot control. Knowing which is which is freeing and helps decrease the tension in a household. What we CAN do is simply provide the boundaries and environment: we cannot "make" them nap and we do not "make" them eat. But there are things we can do to make this adventure enjoyable and feel much more successful. Let's go there next!

Feeding

Food is fun! Mealtimes are when we socialize and relax. This is the atmosphere we can create for our toddlers. However, mealtime can turn into a power play very quickly. If you are having trouble with meal times, then we need to back up and take the stress out first. Feeding is more about atmosphere than about food. If the atmosphere is low stress and positive, then children are much more likely to eat well. If we are in their faces and forcing them to finish five bites, then they will associate mealtime with stress and negative emotions.

o RELAX, RELAX, RELAX!
o Treat this like the normal daily event that it is. No need to over-celebrate every bite.
o Give them freedom to explore their food.
o Be flexible because this WILL get messy and that is OK.
o Toddlers have a 10-15 minute mealtime tolerance window so do not try to contain them for much longer than that. (See the Going out to eat section for tips for that specific feeding situation.)
o Give them freedom to have a varying appetite – sometimes they will want 2 bites and sometimes 20.
o Eat with them as you both face the table.
o Help them with spoon-feeding as needed.
o Give them 2-3 bite-sized bites of food *at a time* on their tray.
o Offer a variety even if they do not like some of it.

- They need full fat foods such as cheese and yogurt. Cook with olive oil, use butter and even try some avocado. They need some fat so they can digest the "fat-soluble" vitamins in their other foods.
- Their tummy is the size of their fist; so keep portions toddler-appropriate.
- Their taste buds are not fully developed. Bitter foods are still off-putting to them. You do not have to make them "love" all those veggies or bitter tastes at this age. It will come on its own. You can however, offer some fun dipping sauces in the meantime.
- Be up to date on your CPR/First Aid.

To reduce the stress of mealtime and reintroduce its rightful place in society and in our households, we have to relax and stop worrying about it. My son Bryce would eat like there was no tomorrow for every fifth meal (it took us a while before we figured out that pattern!-Jen). Give them the freedom to have a variable appetite. Sometimes I am hungry for a steak, and sometimes a salad. Every meal does not have to be a huge food fest.

Our job is to provide the food and it is their job to eat it. We recommend a toddler-sized portion of food for each meal. Give them 2-3 bites of food on the tray at any given time and continue to place additional bites of food on the tray as needed. Snacks are fine but it stays in the kitchen area so they are not running all through the house with food. Then the snack bar closes an hour and a half before suppertime.

Now we have to temper this as in all situations. If your child is not healthy or is not gaining weight, you should enlist the help of a pediatrician or nutritionist. But if your toddler is gaining weight and healthy, give them some reasonable boundaries but make mealtime fun.

They do not need to be the center of attention at every meal. Just relax and determine to enjoy it. Try not to mind the food on the floor; that is messy but fine. Let them explore and have a great time. They will get what they need. And you will be surprised how your household can change when mealtime is not a struggle.

Feeding – Special Circumstances

Won't eat/Picky eater

Follow above guidelines from the previous section. Stop trying to "force" them to eat. It is too stressful. Take a full week when amounts do not matter, the child is sitting facing the table and has three 10-15 minute opportunities to eat at each pre-scheduled meal-time. Offer them 3-4 bites at a time and if they do not eat any of it then the next mealtime will be here in a few hours. Take the stress out and do not focus on them as they eat.

Here is a week-by-week guide

WEEK 1:

If you have been having feeding issues that have made mealtime a chore, then spend a week just making mealtime fun and putting a small variety of nutrient dense foods cut into small bite-sized pieces such as beans, fruits and cheese on their meal tray, 2-3 pieces at time. Then for a whole week, just be OK with whatever they eat and give them about 10 minutes to eat it. The first week is all about LOW STRESS and using a solid schedule that helps them know what to expect, and helps them to be hungry at each meal—which makes a huge difference. We want every advantage we can get.

WEEK 2:

The discovery of the magic sauce. At a few feedings this week, fill a small muffin tray with six food items such as: blueberries, mushed garbanzo beans, soft cheese bits, cereal, soft rice and peas. The other six spaces in the muffin tray are for sauces. Fill the remaining six areas with honey mustard, ketchup, mayo, ranch dressing, yogurt and in the last one put some whipped cream! Then put that tray in front of them and let them have a great mess of a time. Do not face them, do not make stress face.

WEEK 3:
Continue the low stress mealtimes and incorporate nutrient dense foods into the regular menu. Use the secret sauce discovered in week 2 to make some of the healthy options more palatable. Have fun! Your job is to provide the food and the atmosphere. It is their job to eat the food and enjoy the atmosphere.

Throwing sippy cup/food off the tray
Two options
1. Get over it
Toddlers throw stuff off of highchairs. Even if we do not address it, it will resolve once they get a chance to watch us at mealtime and become a part of the family supper routine. They will learn this on their own even if we do not address it.

2. Fix it
If you cannot stand the throwing of the food/sippy cup, or they throw all of their meals off the tray and only want snacks, then we can address it with a three point teaching technique.
#1- Keep your food/sippy cup on the tray.
#2 - If you throw it again, then suppertime is over.
#3 - What I want you to do, is eat like Mommy and Daddy, you'll figure it out." And when that next bite hits the floor, suppertime is over and breakfast comes in the morning.
We may need to institute three mealtimes each day that are in the highchair and very little, if any, snacks. If the food gets thrown we say "If you are throwing food then you must not be hungry so you can get down and breakfast/lunch/supper
144

will be the next feeding time". Say it pleasantly, no stress face and if you are consistent and do not allow any snacks but wait until the next mealtime to place 2-3 bites of food at a time on their tray, they will get the picture in a couple of mealtimes and we are done and can reinstitute snack times.

If it is the sippy cup that keeps hitting the floor, you can take it by itself and put it in the fridge until later. They will not starve. Now we have to temper this as in all situations; if your child is not healthy or gaining weight, you should enlist the help of a pediatrician or nutritionist. But if your toddler is gaining weight and healthy, give them some reasonable boundaries but make mealtime fun and low-stress.

Whining about snack choices
"You get what you get and you don't pitch a fit." If the whining continues snack time is over and we find something else to do.

What if I, as the parent, tend to obsess about food and food choices?
Relaxing is the key! YOUR CHILD WILL EAT MUCH BETTER IN A RELAXED AND FUN FEEDING ATMOSPHERE. Your job is to provide a variety of food and their job is to eat it. Let them have an unhealthy snack on occasion. It is OK. Their taste buds mature as they get older. We just provide choices, even ones they seem not to like so the opportunity is there when those taste buds mature.

What if my child will only eat one or two foods?
Patience is key. They do go through seasons of preferring one food or one color food. We still offer a variety of foods and make it fun. Do not ask them if they WANT peas. Put peas on their tray and then have some on your plate as well.

Let them watch *you* eat them like a normal person, don't overdo it. You cannot force them to eat. Those peas will keep showing up on the tray at mealtime here and there. That is extent of what you really have control over.

"This is what we are having for lunch. You are going to love trying new things." (We know full well that they do NOT love trying new things, but if WE don't believe it and communicate it, they will not believe it either.)
This is not a "quick fix," six months down the road, they will realize that they really do like peas, even if it does have ketchup on it.

My child hates mealtime
This is typically the result of either keeping them in the high chair for too long, trying to get them to eat portions that are too large or creating a stressful feeding environment. De-stress mealtime. Shorten it to 10-15 minutes and offer a portion the size of their fist.
Never ask them if they WANT to eat, tell them it is time to eat. "It is time for supper, your seat is right here. We love to eat with you!"
Avoid stress-face at mealtimes!

Child will not eat meals and only wants sugary treats
It is our job to provide three meals and two healthy snacks. The other stuff is extra and at our discretion. "No Oreos today sweetheart, your choice is fruit or yogurt. I love how fun it is to eat the yogurt off the spoon!"

Anytime in any of these scenarios that things escalate to a tantrum, mealtime is over and Simmer Time begins. They need to simmer. And once they come out of Simmer Time, we tell them that, "You were in Simmer Time because you

146

needed some time to simmer down. We are going to enjoy eating together, we really are sweetheart."

Depending on the time and atmosphere, they can go back in the high chair to try again. We only "try again" once. If another tantrum ensues, then mealtime is over and we get to eat again at the following mealtime. Although this sounds harsh, the outcome is that they figure it out in a couple of days and we are not worrying about it anymore. If we really set up some clear boundaries for a few days, they settle right into new habits that help them to eat better and help mealtime to be less stressful.

GENERAL CHEAT SHEETS

Proverbs 22:6
Train up a child in the way he should go,
And when he is old he will not depart from it.

Putting It All Together

We are finally ready to put everything that we learned into practice. We do realize that many of you have skipped to this section without reading the basic principles that we set forth in the beginning of this book and we forgive you. We would have done that too. But we cannot stress the importance of getting a great foundation laid before starting to build your house. So, refer to the full explanations included in the book to get the best understanding of how to use these helpful principles.

When we have the overall structure in place, every boundary stone settled in a dependable spot, our children really thrive. We can't wait for them to surprise you with what they are really capable of doing!

We originally discussed the boundary stones so that we could set up a structure whereby we could keep from pulling out all our parental hair and maybe on some days even have time to shower. But well beyond that, these things have extraordinary value. They are the building blocks for great character. In the next section, we give you quick tips on how to put all of the things that you have learned into practice so that you can keep these boundaries in place as much as reality allows and see the following returns for years to come.

Boundary Stones

Keys to Character Building

We are finally ready to put everything that we learned into practice and begin our quest to be more effective and less frustrated parents with a plan! This will build the above character traits while helping to keep our household manageable and give us more time to laugh and love our time with our toddlers. Moms on Call is dedicated to providing specific and practical tools that address the realities of life.

The following section will get you started and give you everyday examples of what to say and what to do. And before you know it, you will no longer need the script or the specific direction, it will all start to come naturally.

How to Use the Cheat Sheets

Each Cheat Sheet is broken down into sections.

TRUTH

The basic foundation which will determine our actions.

IN THE MOMENT

This is a guideline on what to say and do "in the moment" or when the challenging behavior is occurring. You can adjust these to fit your personality just keep it short, simple, positive and say it with "confident face".
We also cover how to utilize the Three Point Teaching Technique when appropriate.

Three Point Teaching Technique Review
- o   1. Identify the unwanted behavior
- o   2. State the consequence
- o   3. Teach the desired behavior
- o   Once you have followed through with the consequence: Always follow-up with a {HUG}
  - **H** - **H**old them close,
  - **U** - **U**se confident face and
  - **G** - **G**ive positive feedback {HUG}

TRIANGULATION

This is what to say to loved-ones while your child is in the room. Use these at dinnertime or when you are dropping your toddler off at a babysitter/grandparent's house. They will love it!

This is what to say right before bed. Our full nighttime routines are listed in the "Sleep" section of this book. Once we have stated the household rules and gone over something the child did well, then it is time to cover the "One thing we are working on." This is the "one thing we are working on" statement.

We can only address one issue per night. It may take several nights of repeating the same thing before it begins to "click" for them. They learn by repetition. So, once they master "Getting in the car seat" you can move on to using the *Between awake and asleep* statement for "potty training" or whatever behavior that you are going to work on next.

AVOID

These are common pitfalls and tendencies that undermine our success in each specific situation.

Some more tips about using the cheat sheets:
We have to address issues one at a time with toddlers, we cannot fill their day with ten 'Triangulations' and cover five "things we are working on " right before bed. Just one at a time, ease into it. When you are ready to tackle each issue, the cheat sheets are here to help you get started.

The order that we like to handle unwanted behaviors:
- o   Establish all night sleep
- o   Address feeding issues
- o   Things that hurt your toddler or hurt others
- o   Things that frustrate you in order of how irritating they are for you.

Getting Rid of the Pacifier Cheat Sheet

There is only one real time to get rid of the pacifier and that is WHEN YOU ARE READY (preferably sometime before the 2nd birthday).

TRUTH

My child can live and thrive without the pacifier. He/She/They can do it! It will take a 3-5 day adjustment complete with a few tantrums and extra crying at naptimes, but they can do it!!

IN THE MOMENT

What to say:
"You don't need the paci anymore. You will be just fine. Let's play with your blocks/puzzles/etc...".

What to do:
- Get rid of all the pacis—just throw them away. The child does not watch that happen. Throw them away when the child is asleep.
- Trust in the truth.
- When they ask for the paci, repeat the above phrase word-for-word (or a 2-sentence equivalent of your choosing) as many times as needed.
- At naptime, they go down for a nap at the same time/environment as usual. The naptime may be difficult for 5-7 days but stay consistent. See naptime instructions.
- Be clear, confident and consistent. Your face is confident and your tone is matter-of-fact.

154

TRIANGULATION

"_____(insert child's name) is such a big kid and does not need that paci anymore. She/He is totally going to rock this paci-free stuff. Just wait, you'll see"

BETWEEN AWAKE AND ASLEEP

"You are going to be so great at sleeping without that paci. I love you, I believe in you and I will see you when the sun comes up."

AVOID

o Giving in
o Trying to reason with them
o Explaining why they do not have the paci anymore
o Putting "OK" at the end of sentences "You don't need the paci anymore, OK?"
o Making stress face. (This simply communicates that you are not sure they can do it.)

The "No" Stage Cheat Sheet

Asserting one's free will is a normal developmental milestone. The good news is if your child is saying "no" frequently, then they are right on track developmentally. The bad news is that it can be frustrating and requires great patience.

TRUTH

This is a normal stage of growth and development. I can use this to help my toddler understand who is in control of the day.

IN THE MOMENT

We cannot do a three-point teaching technique every time our child says "no." We would have no time left in the day.

What to say:
- o Every time your toddler says, "No" you reply, "Not 'No,' 'yes Ma'am' (or Sir) and do it.'"

What to do:
- o Help them to do what you have asked of them as if there is no other option and do it cheerfully.
- o What we want to do is to use this time to clearly establish how things work at our house and we get endless opportunities to place that truth in their heart.
- o This will not make the "no" stop, it will just reset their thinking so that in the future—like after you have said this about 3 million times and they are 3-4 years old—they will automatically know the proper response and they WILL start to respond to it.

- This is just a learning opportunity. We can use this time to instill the wanted response, which will carry them right into pre-teen years. You will get to the point where they will say "No." Then you will raise an eyebrow and they will then self-correct and say "Yes Ma'am" and do it.
- Setting this principle in place helps us build confidence in ourselves while setting the atmosphere for our children simultaneously. Every time we say "Not 'No,' 'Yes Ma'am and do it,'" we set up a framework for how our household runs smoothly. We set up a pattern of instruction that will settle into their hearts.
- We had twins saying "No"! It was free-will carnival each day at our respective houses, so we have been there! The great news is that this really works.

TRIANGULATION

N/A

BETWEEN AWAKE AND ASLEEP

N/A

Whining Cheat Sheet

This is just a way that toddlers learn to communicate with us that gets the desired result. It will decrease if it does not produce the desired result. Our kids will only speak to us in the way we allow them to.

TRUTH

My child can use their sweet voice.

IN THE MOMENT

What to say:
In a very calm and matter-of-fact way say, "I cannot understand what you are saying when you whine. When you talk to me in a calm, soft voice, like I am using now, then I can help you."

What to do:
- You may have to repeat this several times. If they are strong willed, then this may turn into a tantrum in an effort to have their own way and get your attention.
- If your child continues to whine after being told 3 times that you do not understand whining, then you can move on to:

The three-point teaching technique: (they do not have to be looking at you for this to work)
- #1: I do not want you to whine.
- #2: If you continue to speak that way, you will go into Simmer Time and come out when you are ready to speak in a way that I can understand.
- #3: I want you to speak in your regular sweet voice so I can understand what you are saying. I love your sweet voice.

- If the whining continues then off to Simmer Time it is.
- Most importantly, once they calm down, we have a chance to speak to the heart of the matter:
- {HUG} "You can be great at using your sweet voice. It's my favorite!"

TRIANGULATION

"Sometimes ____(insert child's name) speaks in this whiny voice I seriously cannot understand. But I sure do love when ____(child's name) speaks in that sweet voice. That is my favorite and I can hear it every time."

Another option for two-parent family:
Having both parents on the same page will help develop respectful tones from your toddler in this way:
If dad says "We do not speak to Mommy that way. If you continue to do that, I will put you in Simmer Time. What I want you to do is talk to Mommy with sweet voice that she loves. She is our princess and we treat her that way." WOW! Doesn't that just melt your heart?

BETWEEN AWAKE AND ASLEEP

"Whining never works in this house. I love the sound of your sweet voice. I look forward to hearing you use that sweet voice to speak to Mommy/Daddy/Grandma every day. I love you, I believe in you and I will see you when the sun comes up."

AVOID

- Feeling like your child has to be looking at you to hear you
- Allowing a child to emotionally highjack a meal or a family atmosphere

159

- Giving in
- Saying "Don't talk like that, OK?"
- Just saying "Don't do that" (it does not help them develop a better option)
- Avoid giving more than three reminders before you turn it into an actionable three point teaching technique.

NOTE: These guidelines are for healthy children who are sleeping 10-12 hours IN A ROW each night. (If they are not, see sleep section of this resource.)

Tantrums Cheat Sheet

Tantrums are a show and this show is all for you. They only continue if they are effective. If you would like tantrums to stop, then ignore them. And ignoring them means we face it with a confident face and place them in "Simmer Time" so they cannot disrupt the entire household. Our goal is to break the "line of sight". We do not want them to be able to gauge how successful this is by the shades of red that our face is turning. We want to transfer responsibility for this behavior to them where it belongs.

TRUTH

o   If you want a behavior to continue, pay attention to it. – the reverse is very true here.
o   It is OK for toddlers to get frustrated, it is not ok for them to hijack the household atmosphere because of their frustration or treat you poorly because of their frustration.
o   This takes time and consistency. This will not resolve in one "Simmer Time," in 20 minutes or even in one day. It may take many "Simmer Times" before they really learn to manage their own frustrations.
o   The truth is that they are loved, they are safe and they can learn to manage those frustrations.
o   If you are having to read this section multiple times a day then we also want you to:

> o   Make sure the child is sleeping 10-12 hours IN A ROW at night. (If not, see sleep section.)
> o   They are healthy.
> o   That you are setting aside time each day for playtime with your child. Playtime that is not instructional but just plain fun.

What to say:

- Say calmly and firmly, "Not in this house" or "We don't play that" or "Looks like you need some alone time to simmer down."

What to do:

- Place the child in a safe, non-threatening environment where they cannot follow you and then you walk away. (See Simmer Time section.)
- This will elicit louder screaming at first but do not give in. They can settle down and they will if they do not get any response from you.
- They learn pretty quickly whether tantrums will work, so although it gets worse before it gets better, it will get much better when we 'nip this in the bud.
- Tantrums need to be ignored and toddlers need to be put in a safe place where they can work out that frustration—separate from you and your concerned eyebrows.
- This is not a teachable moment. It is not time to do a three point teaching technique.
- When "placing them in a safe environment," they may go double-jointed on you and slip right out of your grasp when are trying to pick them up. You can then grasp them firmly at the waist and place them under your arm in a sideways position to carry them to a safe place. Do this silently. Try to stay in control and act as if this does not affect you in any way.
- Place them in a safe area and walk away. Remember, this is not a teachable moment.
- They are looking for a response from you. They are in the business of getting us right to the brink of frustration because "giving in" is not far behind.
- As you place them in Simmer Time, it is the perfect time to pull out that "Confident Face" that you practiced in the mirror.

- When they go into "Simmer Time," they learn how to settle themselves down from a highly agitated state. And they also learn that tantrums do not get them what they want. This is paramount in a child's life.
- How long do you leave them in there? – See Simmer Time Section.

TRIANGULATION

"_____(insert child's name) really throws a fit sometimes but he/she is going to learn how to wait and how to obey Mommy. It may take some time but I am confident that _____ can do it!"

BETWEEN AWAKE AND ASLEEP

"Today you had a fit and yelled and screamed, but I know that you can listen and do what mommy asks, every time. That's just how you are made. I love you, I believe in you and I will see you when the sun comes up."

AVOID

- Giving in
- Allowing them to hijack the peace of the household atmosphere with a full blown tantrum
- Trying to reason with them or talk to them in the midst of a tantrum
- Trying to make them "look at you" so you can "talk some sense into them"
- Bargaining with them
- Making "concerned" face
- Getting increasingly frustrated yourself
- Making idle threats
- Saying "Stop that, *I mean it*"

NOTE: These guidelines are for healthy children who are sleeping 10-12 hours IN A ROW each night. (If they are not, see sleep section of this resource.)

Special circumstances (with the approval of your pediatrician)

Head banger? This method will decrease the overall number of times your child's head hits the floor. If we give in, then they will do this more often because they will know that it works. Then, the cumulative number of times the head hits the floor will increase exponentially. When you put them in "Simmer Time" try to use a carpeted room.

Breath-holder? This method will decrease the amount of times that your child has breath-holding spells. This is very frightening for parents but once the child passes out, the autonomic nervous system takes over and the body will start the breathing process. If we give in to this behavior, it will only increase in intensity and frequency. (Be up to date on your CPR as a precaution and always have this behavior evaluated by your pediatrician.)

Sleep Cheat Sheet

_____

_____

_____

We recommend reading the previous sleep section of this book in its entirety. Use this cheat sheet as a quick reminder only.

TRUTH

My child is safe, loved and they can learn to do this. My job is to provide time, opportunity and a safe sleep environment. I will believe that they can do this until they catch on.

- Use pull-ups/diaper for nighttime until your child has one full week of staying dry at night.
- We do not take a sippy cup of milk to bed.
- Do not allow any naps to last longer than 2 hours. If they are going to one nap a day then that nap can last 3 hours. Naptime should be over by 4 p.m. at the latest
- Middle of the night feedings – There will not be any and they will not starve.
- **The adult white noise machines are an essential piece of the puzzle. It stays on LOUD all night – white noise only (no nature sounds).**
- If your toddler needs it, you may use a night lite. (We recommend www.goodnitelite.com.)
- We do not sleep train when our child is legitimately sick.
- The child's room is childproofed—completely.
- The lock on the door is switched so it locks from the outside/hallway side.

IN THE MOMENT

Night One:
- The bedtime routine always starts with a bath.

- After the bath, we can play music and just have some fun in their room for 10-15 minutes. Then take down all the stimulation. Dim the lights, or turn on just a lamp.
- This is when we read and prayed with our kids.
- When their heart is most open and receptive, go over the household rules then one great thing they did and one thing we are working on together. "Tonight you are going to get to sleep in your own room and sleep right here in your big kid bed. You are going to be so great at it! Here is how you start; pull up your bed covers, close your eyes and fall asleep. I am going to close the door to keep you safe. I love you, I believe in you and I will see you in the sun comes up."
- Then, white noise goes on, the main light goes off and the door closes.
- The door opens again in the morning regardless of pleas of any type, manipulative statements or crying. This way, you said that you believed in them and you put action behind your words.
- Do not go in the room and intervene unless you need to save them from getting hurt.

Night Two:
- After reading 1-2 books, go over the household rules and then say: "Last night when you got to sleep (even if they ended up crying and fell asleep in front of the door), you slept in your room all night and then we saw each other in the morning just like I said we would. Tonight, I want you to stay in your bed, pull up your covers, close your eyes and go right to sleep. I love you, I believe in you and I will see you when the sun comes up."
- Then turn on the white noise, turn off the main light and close the door.
- "No engagement policy" until the door opens at the same time each morning

Night Three:
- Go over the same routine and say the same things that you said on night two. Go over the household rules, let them know that you believe in them.
- If they are playing with toys, pulling out the clothes from their closet or behaving poorly after you leave the room at night, do not go in the room and intervene unless you need to save them from getting hurt. We deal with these things in the morning
- They do not need to play, they need to get right to sleep and if you keep going in the room to sort out poor behavior, then they are not going to do what we know they can do: get to sleep.
- We are not doing three point teaching techniques here. We are just sending consistent messages and backing up our words with our actions. They will get it.
- White noise is on LOUD, then turn off the light and get out and close the door.
- "No engagement policy" until the door opens at the same time each morning.

Night Four:
- Same routine as all other nights.
- If the previous night, they did not go right to sleep then after the statement of the household rules, remind them that you know they will be great sleepers and they can sleep in their own bed like a champ.
- If they did well the night previous then be sure to mention it like you knew they could do it all along. "Last night you did just like Mommy said. You pulled up your covers, closed your eyes and went to sleep. I am so proud of you. I knew you would be great at this. Now, you know just how to do it. I love you, I believe in you and I will see you when the sun comes up."
- Get out and close the door.
- There is a "No engagement policy" until the door opens at the same time each morning.

Continue this routine until we are having regular nights of consistent sleep. It may be emotionally exhausting but worth it on so many levels. They will go to bed knowing that you believe in them, you support them and that you do what you say you are going to do.

TRIANGULATION

"_____(Insert Child's name) is going to sleep all night in his/her/their comfy bed and be great at it. I am not worried. _____(child's name) is going to sleep all night in their room. Just wait."

AVOID

- Going back in their room or sleeping on their floor
- Talking to them through the door
- Staying in the room until they fall asleep
- Unlocking the door or using a locked door as a punishment. "If you stay in your bed then I will not lock the door". That sets them up to think that safety is a punishment.
- Sitting outside the door
- Letting them sleep in your room
- Letting them "sleep in" in the morning
- Doing stress-face at night or in the morning
- Parenting out of fear
- Thinking that you do not need to read the ENTIRE sleep section of this book

Transferring to a Toddler Bed Cheat Sheet

TRUTH

Your child can sleep in a toddler bed, in their room, all night and be great at it! Where the crib once limited access to the room, now a door limits access to a whole house.

IN THE MOMENT

What to say:
- o "You can do this."
- o "I believe in you."
- o "You are so brave"
- o I love you so much that I want you to learn to sleep like a big kid."
- o "We close the door to keep you safe."
- o "I love you, I believe in you and I will see you when the sun comes up"

What to do:
- o The first night that your child transitions to the new bed, have your routine ready and their room completely child-proofed – they may explore it a bit as they figure this out. See "sleep section" for details.
- o Give the child/children a bath.
- o Dress the child in their pajamas while playing soft music and dim the lights.
- o Read them a book (two maximum; have them picked out already). At the end of book #2, make a positive statement such as "Okay, it's time for bed and I am going to be in the living room and you are going to stay in this bed like a big kid and fall asleep. You are so good and brave and I can't

wait to see you in the morning. I love you, I believe in you and I will see you when the sun comes up" Do not linger.

o Be ready! This statement may induce a crying fit or a barrage of manipulation. The child may try to talk you out of leaving the room, or try to follow you out of the room. We must get out anyways. They are simply responding to the newness and unfamiliarity of it. They can adjust and they will.

o We leave and **close the door**. It is locked from the hallway side – See "Sleep" section of this book.

o Once that door is closed it does not open until it is time to start the next day. It opens when the sun comes up just like you said it would.

o **Stay out and do not engage in conversation or direction of any type.** That is our entire job at night. It is the hardest thing you have ever had to do thus far. But we will tell our hearts the truth.

The truth is:
They are safe.
They are loved.
They can learn to do this.

o THIS IS CRUCIAL! The next morning, we start the day at the same wake-up time (7 a.m.), even if we have to wake them up. And it is at this time that we use our confident face to redirect any behaviors from the night before. "You didn't have to sleep on the floor when you can sleep in that comfy bed all night and be great at it. You will figure this out. Let's start our day"

TRIANGULATION

"___ is awesome at figuring out this big kid bed. Before we know it, he will be just like us, he will lay down in that bed and go right to sleep and sleep all night."

170

BETWEEN AWAKE AND ASLEEP

"This is your new bed. You are going to be great at sleeping right here all night long. We keep the door closed to keep you safe. I love you, I believe in you and I will see you when the sun comes up."

AVOID

- o In a multiple child household, avoid "saving" the quiet one. Siblings have an innate ability to sleep through loudness. But if another child wakes, they can get themselves back to sleep without our help and will do so better without us in the room offering up extra stimulation in the middle of the night.
- o Feeling like you need to address them through the door. We will address any unwanted nighttime behavior—in the morning. See "Sleep" section of this book and read it in its entirety.
- o Underestimating how well your toddler can adjust given time and a solid routine.
- o Letting your toddler come sleep with you.
- o Talking yourself into engaging them just "one more time". They do not need to talk to you, go potty, have a drink of water or come out of their room. Nighttime is the time to stay in their room and they will be great at it.

Naptime Cheat Sheet

Naptime becomes a "nap opportunity" they may cry, play or sleep but our job is to provide a great sleep environment free of added stimulation and it is their job to sleep. Sometimes they will, sometimes they won't. They can stay in their child-proofed room for an hour and a half minimum.

The primary concept that helps to reduce tension in the household (and in our hearts) is knowing what things are our responsibility. We can clearly tell our child when naptime begins; we can turn on the white noise, make it nice and cool in the room and give them kisses. Then we can close the door and open it 1 ½ to 3 hours later. But we cannot make them sleep. That is their job.

TRUTH

They may not be able to get to sleep every day. On the days that we are home, we provide the great sleep environment and consistent times and they will sleep some days, cry some days and play some days.

IN THE MOMENT

What to say:
   o "It is time for nap. You will be the best napper ever! You will stay in your room until naptime is over and Mommy comes to get you." (confident face, no other options, close the door and lock it until naptime is over). Room must be childproofed.

What to do:

- o Back up your statement with action. Let them cry, play or sleep but they stay in their room for the designated amount of time. For example, if you are at one nap a day then it is 1 ½ hours minimum and 3 hours maximum. (These are from the start of the naptime, not the time they actually fell asleep.) So if they went into the nap at noon then they are out of the nap at 1:30 if they are awake and out of the nap at 3 pm even if we have to wake them.
- o If you are consistent, this will become part of their routine and they typically will unwind or get themselves to sleep. They will have times, when their boundary stones are out of place, that they will test you to see if this naptime boundary stone has moved. It does not mean that they do not need a nap, it means that you have an opportunity to keep their lives in control and keep that boundary in place so they will ultimately feel secure.
- o Toddlers occasionally have a week of interrupted sleep at naptime as they reach certain developmental milestones. This will sort itself out, keep naptime consistent even when they are not responding by sleeping consistently.
- o Please note: Naptimes are much more difficult to establish when nighttime is not solid. Meaning that children who sleep 10-12 hours in a row per night will have much, much better naptimes.
- o There are also further guidelines about ages and times in the "naptime" section of this resource.

TRIANGULATION

"____(insert child's name) is the best napper ever!" or "I love it when ___(child's name) sleeps for naptime, their body just needs it and they are so great at it"

"You are a great sleeper. I love that and I love you, I believe in you and I will see you when the sun comes up."

AVOID

- o   Over-explaining
- o   Saying "It's naptime....OK?"
- o   Skipping naptime when you are home because you are overwhelmed (the nap will be the most helpful thing for you both)
- o   Sitting outside the door or being glued to the monitor (this is your free time-use it)
- o   Making the naptime optional dependent upon your toddler's mood/approval.
- o   Letting them go to bed early because they skipped a nap (this undermines the next day's nap).

Instructions for special circumstances:

- o   **Won't stay in their room?** Close the door and lock it from the outside.

- o   **Room is not safe?** Childproof it thoroughly.

- o   **Won't sleep?** They can cry, play or sleep. They get a "nap opportunity" at the same time each day.

- o   **Don't like any of these options?** You are the parent. You can run your day in the way that you best see fit.

Feeding Cheat Sheet

Feeding is much more about ATMOSPHERE than it is about food. More information about special feeding challenges is addressed in the feeding section of this book. We recommend reading that section in its entirety.

TRUTH

It is my job to provide the food; it is their job to eat it.

IN THE MOMENT

What to say:
- Set the atmosphere
  - o "I love eating with you."
  - o "Time for US to have lunch."
- During mealtime
  - o "These beans are delicious. I really enjoy eating them."
  - o "I love the way broccoli makes that crunch noise when I eat it. That is fun."

What to do:
- o RELAX, RELAX, RELAX!
- o Treat this like the normal daily event that it is. No need to over-celebrate every bite.
- o Give them freedom to explore their food
- o Be flexible because this WILL get messy and that is OK.
- o Toddlers have a 10-15 minute mealtime tolerance window, so do not try to contain them for much longer than that. (See 'Going out to eat' section for that specific feeding situation.)

- Give them freedom to have a varying appetite –sometimes they will want 2 bites and sometimes 20.
- Eat with them as you both face the table.
- Help them with spoon-feeding as needed.
- Give them 2-3 bite-sized bites of food at a time on their tray.
- Offer a variety even if they do not like some of it.
- Don't forget to include full-fat foods such as full fat cheese, yogurt, butter, cook in olive oil and let them try some avocado. These kids need some natural fats to digest the "fat soluble" vitamins in the rest of their food.
- Their tummy is the size of their fist, so keep portions toddler-appropriate.
- Help your child become interested in what you are eating instead of putting the attention on what they are not eating.
- Know what to do if your child is choking. Be up to date on your CPR/First Aid.

TRIANGULATION

"Mealtime is such a fun time to be together and explore new foods _____(Insert child' name) is going to be great at enjoying family mealtime."

BETWEEN AWAKE AND ASLEEP

"It is my job to provide the food and your job to eat it and you will be great at it"

AVOID

- Making stress-face
- Sitting face to face the entire meal

176

- Putting too much emphasis on mealtime
- *Over*-celebrating each bite (you do not celebrate when your husband takes a bite of food)
- Requiring a certain number of bites
- Only offering foods that they will eat
- Freaking out about a mess or at all for that matter
- Feeling responsible for every bite
- Putting them on an adult – low-fat diet
- Offering too much food at one time
- Over-explaining why they need to eat
- Being nutrition-obsessed (conscious is fine but not obsessed)

NOTE: These guidelines are for healthy children, if you are concerned about your child's growth and development check with your pediatrician. Although, these guidelines, when used in conjunction with your pediatrician/dietician's recommendations, can be quite helpful.

Going Out to Eat Cheat Sheet

Toddlers have about a 10-15 minute mealtime tolerance window. So we do not expect them to sit indefinitely while we enjoy long conversation and two cups of coffee. We can, however, make going out to eat a more enjoyable experience. Children want to know what you expect and what will happen. Some misbehavior is because they have no idea how long this may last so they want out immediately.

TRUTH

I can enjoy a meal out in public with my family. My children can be a fun part of this time of socialization and celebration.

IN THE MOMENT

What to say:
Prior to going into the restaurant, while you are still in the car:
- o "We are going in to eat. Here is what will happen, we will sit down at the table and you can play with your toy/book.
- o Then we order our food and just before the food comes, we will take a little walk.
- o Then the food comes and we eat and when we are done you can play some more and we will leave.
- o Don't forget our household rules apply here.
- o "We love going out together as a family." (You set the atmosphere.)

During the meal
- o "We use our sweet voice in the restaurant."
- o "You are doing a great job with the coloring."
- o "We will get a field trip in a few minutes."
- o "Let's go see the plants in the front of this place."

- o "Time to go potty." (bring the wipes)
- o "Our food is here! Let's eat."

What to do:
- o Go to a **family-friendly** restaurant
- o Ask the waiter to let you know a few minutes before the food is supposed to arrive.
- o Let things follow the plan that you state in the "what to say" section above.
- o Right before the food comes, take your child for a little walk. You can go to the potty, you can go outside and look at the shrubs or you can take a little tour and show your toddler: where you go to pay, what door the waiters go thru to get the food and point out interesting things like light fixtures or wall art. No free-roaming.
- o Then go back to your seat and finish your mealtime.
- o When the food arrives, ask for the check.
- o Remember that toddlers will not tolerate endless conversation. So if you want to go out for a long discussion and several cups of coffee, get a babysitter.
- o We simply do the best we can to put these boundaries in place.

TRIANGULATION

"_____(insert name of child) can be so much fun to be with at a restaurant. _____(name of child) is going to get the hang of what family time looks like in public."

BETWEEN AWAKE AND ASLEEP

"When we go out to eat together, it is our fun family time and Daddy and I love to talk together and we love it when you are with us. You will get better and better at sitting still and enjoying that time with us. I love you, I believe in you and I'll see you when the sun comes up."

- o Putting them in the "seat of no attention" (let them participate in conversation and attention)
- o Putting them in a seat that they can get out of
- o Endless conversation
- o Forcing them to eat (see feeding section)
- o Rolling your eyes and giving an exasperated sigh every 3 minutes
- o Saying negative things about this experience
- o Reacting to the facial expressions of other patrons of the restaurant

Fast Food Tips:
- o If you are going to a fast food restaurant that has a play yard then let your child play first.
- o This is a great spot for you to relax and allow your child to play.
- o Do not get into a power play over three chicken nuggets and force your child to eat them before going on the playground.
- o The food often comes in a box or bag so you can take it home and eat it later.
- o If you are saying to yourself that your child would not eat at all unless you make them eat first, then refer to the feeding section of this book. It does not matter if your child misses out on three chicken nuggets and some fries.
- o Have a nutritious dinner that night or let them snack on the fries on the way home.
- o Do not sit them right next to children having fun on a playground and force them to eat fried foods. Let them play and take the food with you when you go.
- o This is a break for YOU.

Hitting/Biting Cheat Sheet

TRUTH

My child can treat others well. He/she is indicating that they need a very clear and immediate boundary in this situation.

IN THE MOMENT

What to say:
- Get very close to their face and startle them with the firm and loud tone—not yelling but firm and loud enough to catch them off guard. "YOU DO NOT HIT/BITE"
- Face is stern and serious but controlled and calm.

What to do:
- Place them in immediate "Simmer Time." (See Simmer Time guidelines.)

- {**HUG**} "This is important. You got put in Simmer Time because you hurt someone else and we are ____(insert last name) and ___(last name) are good to people. Don't do that again." Say that with your eyebrows raised like you mean it.

TRIANGULATION

"___(insert child's name) IS going to learn how to treat others with kindness and she/he will be great at it."

"You do not slap at Mommy's face or hit another child because you are a ____(insert last name) and we are good to people."

AVOID

- ○ Freaking out
- ○ Asking them "why" they are hitting
- ○ If they hit you and then look at you as if this is a game put them right in simmer time, avoid looking back at them as if they are cute in this moment
- ○ Making excuses for their behavior
- ○ Negotiating
- ○ Tolerating being hit or bitten
- ○ Being afraid that your child will bite forever (they won't)

NOTE: These guidelines are for healthy children who are sleeping 10-12 hours IN A ROW each night. (If they are not, see sleep section of this resource.)

Putting on Jacket/Shoes Cheat Sheet

Review the 'Don't miss this' section. It is ok to expect that your toddler will respond to the schedule of the day.

TRUTH

The schedule of the day works best when an adult is in charge. My child can put on their non-optional outerwear.

IN THE MOMENT

What to say:
- "It's time to get dressed and you will be great at it."
- "We are putting on your jacket now. This will be fun!"
- "How many shoes are we putting on? Two? Perfect. On they go."

If they take these items off while outside at playtime
- "Oh, I see you took your shoes off, that means it's time to go back inside." (And then take them inside, wait for the tantrum to be over and then) {**HUG**} "I see you still want to be outside, you can put your shoes on and keep them on and be great at it. Inside, Outside, you always have to obey Mommy, that's just how it works."

If they are still in a huff and refusing
- Shrug your shoulders and repeat (without anger), "Inside, outside, you always have to obey Mommy, that's just how it works. You'll figure it out."
- Do not let them back outside until they have their shoes back on. But we do not need to take it to the extreme. Just work on it each day and do your best to make reasonable boundaries for their behavior.

- o If you need to get out the door to school. Make it non-optional. Put their shoes on and get in the car.

What to do:
- o Give clear direction.
- o Use 2-3 sentences only.
- o Pleasantly help them to comply as if there is no other option because there is not another option.
- o Make sure that their clothing is not ill-fitting or limiting their ability to run and play.

TRIANGULATION

"When it is time for us to go, we go. _____(Insert name) is going to be great at putting on their clothing/shoes."

BETWEEN AWAKE AND ASLEEP

"When Mommy says to put on your jacket/shoes, it's time to do it and you are going to be so great at getting dressed just like Mommy and Daddy do every day, you will totally get it. I love you, I believe in you and I will see you when the sun comes up."

AVOID

- o Putting 'OK' at the end of non-optional events
- o Asking them if they "want to."
- o Giving them too many choices.
- o Over explaining the reasons why they have to wear shoes (they don't care).
- o Trying to coax, convince or reason with them.

Going to the Grocery Store Cheat Sheet

No need to dread this part of everyday life. Here are some tips to make it a much better experience.

We have a strict "no free-roaming" policy. But once they are in that little grocer buggy, we cannot expect them to sit in the "seat of no attention" for 45 minutes while we shop. We have to make this fun and interactive.

Remember if your toddler cries, it is more likely that other people understand, than that they are annoyed. Either way, **you are not responsible for strangers perceived opinions; you are responsible for your child.**

TRUTH

I can enjoy my child's presence at everyday activities like food shopping. I will make them part of the process and determine to have fun.

IN THE MOMENT

What to say:
(In the car prior to getting out)
- We are at the store and our household rules apply here. When Mommy says "No" I mean "No." I love being here with you. This is fun.

(While shopping)
- You are my helper today, which apple is green?
- Which bananas are the best ones?
- Here, you can put this in the cart.

- This coupon has a picture of a Green Giant, can you point to the can with this picture on it?

If they are whining for an item you do not intend to purchase:

- "You get what you get and you don't pitch a fit." (That is the official southern version.) Then distract them with another helper activity or option.

What to do:

- As often as it is possible, choose the ideal time to go to the store. Behaviorally speaking, that is mid-morning.
- Place your child in the proper seat.
- There is a strict "No free roaming" policy when in public places.
- It is not advisable to allow your toddler to walk through the store on their own. They may want to get down but if we can enlist their help right away, they will often stay put.
- Make them a part of the process.
- Pick up colorful vegetables and ask them which one should go in the cart (even if it is not your first choice).
- Drive the buggy close enough to the produce so they can pick out an apple and drop it in the buggy.
- Select two cans of green beans and let your toddler pick which one goes in the buggy.
- If you have coupons, let them help you to look for the color product that matches the coupon. (Do not let them to "hold" the coupons.)
- When you say "no," mean it and move on.

Three-point teaching technique (If they are pushing the envelope and putting up a fight or tantrum)

- #1 "You cannot scream for items that you want."
- #2 "Continuing to do this will not result in you getting your way."
- #3 "What I want you to do is to sit here quietly and help Mommy pick out the next item on our list."

- If the unwanted behavior continues then keep shopping, use distraction (tip: making vegetable friends is fun!) and try to get them involved in the grocery shopping process. This may be a noisy endeavor, and that is okay!
- But don't forget the most important step after a consequence - {HUG}: The positive statement should be "Hey, we can get through this grocery store without any outbursts. We can do it! I love you, sweetheart" AND MOVE ON.

TRIANGULATION

"_____(Insert name of child) is going to be such a pleasure to be with at the grocery store. It is our fun time together and I look forward to it. I love spending time with _____(name of child)."

BETWEEN AWAKE AND ASLEEP

"When we are the grocery store or anywhere outside this house, Mommy helps to keep you safe and it is important to listen to me. I know you will be great at it! I love you, I believe in you and I will see you when the sun comes up!"

AVOID

- Trying to go shopping with your toddler late in the evening or after school when they have just downed two cupcakes at a birthday party
- Giving in. If you give in to the crying or tantrum then you are teaching your toddler to continue that behavior—because it works.
- Letting them roam freely
- Putting them in the "Seat of no attention" for 45 minutes

- Reacting to the facial expressions of the other patrons of the grocery store

Holding Hands Across the Street Cheat Sheet

TRUTH

When their life is at stake, I will hold on to my child whether they like it or not.

IN THE MOMENT

What to say:
- o "We are crossing the street and we hold hands when we cross the street—**every time**."
- o (Confident face—pleasant and firm as if there is not another option—and there IS no other option.)

What to do:
- o When you get out of the car with multiple children, always get the baby out first and secure that child in the stroller, then get the toddler out.
- o If you have twin toddlers, get the best-behaved one out first (and you know which one that is).
- o Look both ways and hold their hand firmly as they cross the street
- o If they are not compliant or you feel they are a flight risk, then place your entire hand around their wrist. Hold them firmly until you reach the other side. Even if they go limp, you can get them across without letting go. Keep calm and when you get to the other side you get the {HUG} moment, say, "We hold hands when we cross the street. If you try to let go, Mommy will hold your wrist."

189

- Trying to explain how cars are not looking out for them will not be effective. They really do not understand the result of a huge impact. Just let it be non-optional every time, even if it is a struggle.

TRIANGULATION

"I love holding ____(insert child's name) hand, especially when we cross the street, that's just the way we do it, every time."

BETWEEN AWAKE AND ASLEEP

"One way that we keep you safe is to hold hands when we cross the street. That's just how we do it —every time. I love you, I believe in you and I will see you when the sun comes up."

AVOID

- Over-explaining
- Negotiating
- Free roaming
- Putting 'OK' on the end of this non-optional activity
- Getting the toddler out first, if you have more than one child
- Trusting that they will just "stay close" to you as you cross the street.

Getting into the Car Seat Cheat Sheet

The biggest struggle with the car seat tends to be if we negotiate or stall. It can easily turn into a war of the wills. The trick is to get them into the seat right away, even if it is a struggle and then let the "Triangulation" and "Meeting them between awake and asleep" help them to settle into a better routine.

TRUTH

My child will do what I allow them to do. I am the parent and I run the schedule because that just makes sense. My child can get in their car seat when it is time to go.

IN THE MOMENT

What to say:
- "Time to go, let's start our engines and get out of here. Straight to the car seat we go!"
- "When Mommy/Daddy says it's time to go, then it's time to go."

What to do:
- BE READY. WHEN YOU SAY IT IS TIME TO GO— LET IT REALLY BE TIME TO GO. Do not say this when you still have 5 minutes of talking or gathering items. It sends mixed messages.
- Once you say it then shuffle them out the door with a smile. Repeat, "Straight to the car seat."
- If you have a baby, whenever safe and possible, put the toddler in the car seat first and then attach the baby into their car seat. This helps to prevent the toddler from

191

getting into the car and free-roaming into places that we cannot reach them.

- If you need to place the toddler in their car seat, physically, then do it with a smile and a non-optional confident face. Sometimes this can be like a rodeo complete with flailing limbs. We will address this in triangulation and between awake and asleep

TRIANGULATION

"____(Insert Child's name) is great at getting right into that car seat when it's time to go. I really think they have a superhero skill. They get in that car seat so fast. It's amazing."

BETWEEN AWAKE AND ASLEEP

"You are going to be great at getting in that car seat. It has a lot of straps but you can sit there while Mommy gets them all in place. I love you, I believe in you and I will see you when the sun comes up."

AVOID

- Saying its time to go BEFORE you are ready
- Giving the toddler "free-roaming time" inside the vehicle or outside the vehicle
- Negotiating
- Making stress face
- NEVER. NEVER. NEVER let them ride in the car outside of a car seat. They will want to do that every time and you will regret it.

Riding in the Car Seat Cheat Sheet

TRUTH

It is my job to provide a safe riding environment and their job to learn to enjoy the ride!

My child is buckled securely and cannot go anywhere no matter how much noise they make. They will figure this out with time and opportunity. I can deal with this when their heart is open for instruction AND when I am not driving

IN THE MOMENT

What to say:
  o You'll figure out how to enjoy the ride! You really will. (even in the face of their screaming fit, we will believe in things that are not as if they ARE).

What to do:
  o If they are screaming, turn up the radio and repeat the above phrase mostly for your own benefit; they really won't hear it over their own screaming.
  o Sometimes they just want your attention every few minutes and cannot get it in the car seat because you are facing away from them (as you should be if you are driving). In that instance, try a "verbal game" that lets them know you are still paying attention to them. Something like "When I say Mommy, you say love you" Then say "mommy" and they say "love you". Repeat that a few times. "When I say Grampie, you say silly". Then say "Grampie" and they say "silly". Repeat that a few times. It

helps to have a fun game like this that allows you to watch the road.

Before you get them into the car:
- Make sure the car seat is comfortable and there is not a toy or piece of plastic protruding in an uncomfortable spot.
- Toys and snacks will be thrown, so only things that are attached are recommended.
- Attaching a traveling companion (stuffed animal that attaches to the side of the car seat) often makes it seem more friendly back there

TRIANGULATION

"_____(insert name of child) is really going to learn to enjoy riding in the car. Just wait, they will figure it out."

BETWEEN AWAKE AND ASLEEP

"Car trips are so much fun when we are together. You are going to figure out how to enjoy the ride and I can't wait until you do!"

AVOID

- Loosening the 5 point restraint more than two fingers widths away from their chest or legs
- Trying to "manage" their discontent while driving but turning around often while trying to drive
- Turning around to address them while driving
- Speaking to them in the midst of their tantrum (they won't hear you anyways)
- Bribing
- Negotiating
- Letting them know that this flusters you, they will just scream louder

194

Potty Training Cheat Sheet

Try to make this a very positive experience and be patient. The key is to try to communicate that we know they can do this in a clear, confident and **matter-of-fact** way, both when they are successful and when they are not.

TRUTH

My child can learn to pee and poop in the potty. This is a natural part of growth and development. I will not freak out.

This method is called MOC "Triple P" style. Patience, Persistence, Positivity...followed by peeing and pooping in the potty (Wow! That is a lot of Ps!) Which is what you can expect when you undertake this normal part of growth and development. This Cheat Sheet will give you an overview of how to create a routine that establishes familiarity with the potty and will be successful if we are patient, persistent and positive.

For a more in-depth guide to potty training, including how to personalize the experience for your toddler's SMART design and a weekend method, scan the QR code. Here we go!

When to begin:
- o   Wait until they show interest.
- o   Do not force it.
- o   Let them accompany you in the bathroom so they have an idea of what happens in there.
- o   Typically, between 18 months to almost 3 years of age is the potty training continuum.

- If you have tried several methods unsuccessfully then **take 2 weeks off** —go back to pull-ups or diapers and then we start again with the stress-free instructions below. This will not ruin everything. Start with encouraging them before bed and in front of loved ones that they "Will figure this out" and you "Are not worried" for one week and then utilize the "How to Begin" guidelines below.

How to begin:
- Prepare the bathroom with a basket of books. If possible, be sure that *you* have somewhere to sit. You can even bring younger siblings in the bathroom in their car seat or bouncer. An **empty** bathtub makes for a great place to distract a younger sibling as long as they are never left unattended.
- Use the actual potty with a toddler adapter for the seat.
- Start to use big kid underwear and/or a waterproof training pant for the daytime.
- Pull-ups or diapers for naptime and nighttime are recommended until they wake up dry for at least a week in a row. (This may not happen until between 3 ½-5 years of age.) We do not potty train at naptime or nighttime.
- Put Potty on the schedule about 4-5 times a day at the same time. This will be "potty time." We do not ask them if they need to go. We TELL them that it is "Time to go potty". We simply provide regular, predictable opportunities *for* them to go.
- Help the child pull down their underwear/waterproof training pants if they require your help. Let them do it on their own if they are able.
- Allow child to sit on the potty chair (girls and boys). Boys may take several months to a year before they are standing to pee.
- Be patient. Even if they said they have to go, it can take a few minutes to get the water works moving.
- Stay in the bathroom until they are done or no longer than 5 minutes.

- We are shooting for about a 60% success rate for the first week or so, then 80% and then only an occasional accident.
- Children will usually get the hang of urinating in the potty first. It generally takes longer to be able to adjust to the sensation of pooping in the potty.
- After you have established three or four days of staying dry at least 80% of the time, begin to encourage pooping on the potty. Ask your child to let you know when they have to poop. Sometimes you will have to catch them in the act, usually behind a sofa or in a corner. They will be standing very still and concentrating, making a "poopy face." That is generally a good sign.
- If the child indicates that they have to go potty, get to the potty fast, help them pull down their underwear and stay with them in the bathroom. Keep it low-key but enjoyable.
- They will generally want to get off the potty before having a bowel movement. Encourage them to stay on the potty as long as you can but do not let this escalate into a crying, forcing or begging match. Say, "That's alright, we will try again next time. I am sure that you will be great at pooping in the potty. You will get the hang of it"
- Be prepared as you venture out of the house. Your kids will want to do the grand tour of every bathroom in your town including local grocery stores, restaurants, and gas stations. Bring wipes for the toilets, their hands as well as their bottoms. They will touch stuff that we hoped they wouldn't.
- When they are successful our attitude is a clear, confident "I knew you could do it".
- When they do not poop in the potty, treat them (and yourself) with grace. This is not permanent, they WILL Get the hang of it.

IN THE MOMENT

What to say:
- o "It is Potty time. We are going to the potty and you'll be great at it." (This is not a question; it is a statement.) Clear, confident and in control.

If they have an accident
- o "That's alright, this happens sometimes. You will get the hang of it." Facial expression is relaxed and confident and tone is matter-of-fact.

When they are successful
- o "I knew you could do it." (With a calm, confident smile.)

What to do:
- o Put "Potty Time" into your daily schedule about 4-5 predictable times a day.
- o Stay calm
- o Exude confidence (If they sense that you are stressed or angry about this then they will want to avoid it.)

TRIANGULATION

" _____(insert name of child) is going to get the hang of going in the potty like a big kid. You just wait, _____(name of child) can do this."

BETWEEN AWAKE AND ASLEEP

"You are going to be so great at getting that pee and poop in the potty—the best ever. I love you; I believe in you and I will see you when the sun comes up"

AVOID

o Saying "Do you need to go potty?"
o Saying "We are going potty now, OK?"
o Do not ASK them if they have to go. (Playing is more fun than potty, they will typically say "No" even if they really have to go.)
o The idea is for them to eventually tell you when they have to go, not the other way around.
o VERY IMPORTANT: Do not shame, spank, or insult your child for not pooping or peeing in the potty.
o Do not over-celebrate – no need for the Potty Parade. (This is a natural part of growth and development.)
o Do not make stress face.
o Do not use the Three Point Teaching Technique for potty training.

NOTE: These guidelines are for healthy children who are sleeping 10-12 hours IN A ROW each night. (If they are not, see sleep section of this resource.)

Bringing Home Baby/Sibling Cheat Sheet

TRUTH

This baby or babies are the best thing that ever happened to your
toddler and we are going to treat it as such.
We brought home a baby, not a disease. Life does not revolve
around your toddler; it revolves around the family.
Watching a family serve the youngest and weakest member is a
beautiful and important thing that your toddler gets to be a part
of.

IN THE MOMENT

What to say:
- o "Babies take more of Mommy's time. You will be just fine. "
- o "Babies cry sometimes, it is normal, he/she/they will be just fine"
- o "You can touch her lightly on her feet and arms. You are great at that! You really know how to treat your sister/brother."

What to do:
- o Take the time that you need to serve this baby and get the rest you need.
- o Order the Moms on Call Basic Baby Care resources to set great routines in place that promote rest for everyone.
- o Allow your toddler to help in little ways such as bringing you the diaper bag or a blanket.
- o Treat this like it is the best thing could've happened.
- o Give your household a good month to adjust. Things will seem crazy for a few weeks for everyone; take time to get

adjusted. Enlist others and family members to engage your toddler.

- o Allow him/her/them to broaden their circle of caregivers. This is for a season.
- o Give them time to explore the baby and have time with you and the baby together as much as they are interested.

TRIANGULATION

"I knew -----(insert toddler's name) would be a great big brother/sister. This takes some getting used to but he/she is doing a wonderful job. It is fun to be a family"

BETWEEN AWAKE AND ASLEEP

"Being a big brother or sister takes some getting used to but you are doing a wonderful job. This is what it is like to be a part of a family of __(insert number of people in the household) and we love it, the hard parts and the easy ones."

AVOID

- o Feeling guilty that the world does not revolve around your toddler
- o Underestimating how well your toddler can adjust
- o Making stress face to your toddler all day long because you do not have the same amount of time to give them right now
- o Letting your toddler come sleep with you
- o Feeling solely responsible for everyone's adjustment

Closing Remarks

In the Moms on Call logo, you will find the words: Sleep, Feed, Laugh and Love. We want to talk about leading a balanced life filled with moments of sheer laughter and enjoyment. The entire purpose of this resource is to provide you with more time to actually enjoy your children.

Sleep
Families who enjoy healthy sleep habits are happier, more content, have more time to enjoy the small wonders of life and have a stable foundation in which to handle the regular day-to-day challenges of toddlerhood (not to mention drive a car without being bleary eyed or function at a job!).

Like we said earlier, all of the sleep instructions have a goal in mind. To transform stressful, sleep deprived families that are hanging on for dear life into well-rested confident families who can revel in the sheer delight of family life. We want you to be clear-minded when you are singing to your child before bed, playing with them or reading books, among other things. We even want you to keep your cool when the realities of life hit, like trying to dislodge play-doh from the toilet or getting that bubble gum out of your daughter's beautiful curly locks. Well-rested is always better than tired, curt or irritated. It is a rough road from here to there but what is two weeks in the overall scheme of life?

Feed
The dinner table is a time of togetherness and sharing. We seek to take the stress out of this natural and normal part of

202

life. If there is a perfect time to laugh and play together, then mealtime is one of our favorites. Instead of being so caught up in the number of bites, we would love to have a low-key environment that invites conversation and the occasional use of pretzels as alien antennae. Fun! Fun! Fun! Kids who enjoy and are involved in mealtimes are much better eaters. Don't force it; let it evolve from stress-ridden battles to your favorite time of day by following the guides that are provided for you in this resource.

Laugh

A healthy family life involves a good deal of laughter. **We need time to play with our children that is not "educational" time or "instructional" time**. Just dance, sing and enjoy being together. Freedom! Leave the stress of the workday behind and make a mess, play in the yard, have some hide-and-seek time or break out the tickle monster. We focus on household order so that we can take a break from the activities of daily life, slow down the hustle and bustle and just enjoy the intense blessing and laughter that children bring.

Love

We assume that you are reading this resource because you love your children and desire to really enjoy them. Love comes in many forms. Love as a parent involves providing security and discipline. Love means that we will take on the uncomfortable decisions that we have to make in order to provide a clear structure for the household where our children live and thrive. Peppered throughout this resource, we have an overriding theme of support. Love means believing in our children's ability to do the things that life requires. It is at the core of the three point teaching technique and everything that we recommend. It is why we give "things to say and do," so that families can make order out of chaos and love being together again.

And for even more insight on how to communicate to your toddler, see our Toddler by Design App which breaks down the HUG moments specifically for your toddler's unique personality. It includes tips on sleeping, feeding, tantrums and potty training using your child's specific motivators. Consider it the advanced Moms on Call support resource that personalizes these foundational principles even more. In it you will find our groundbreaking SMART paradigm detailing the top motivators for toddler behaviors and how to understand and utilize their design to influence their behavior in positive ways.

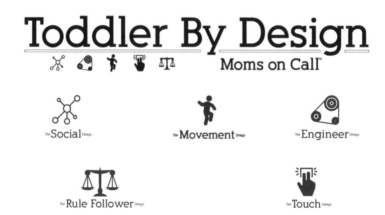

Looking for a curated list of our favorite baby and toddler products?

Scan with your phone's camera or QR Code Reader for quick access to all of the Products We Love that can be shipped straight to your door!

Loved this book and want more?

Our Toddler Online Course compliments this book perfectly, covering our groundbreaking SMART paradigm and so much more. Scan now to continue upping your Toddler communication game!

SLEEP · FEED

MOMS ON CALL

PARENTING THE FIRST 4 YEARS

LAUGH · LOVE

For more Moms on Call resources, please go to momsoncall.com.

Follow us on social media @momsoncall.

More than 750,000 books sold:

Moms on Call: Basic Baby Care (0-6 months)
Moms on Call: Next Steps Baby Care (6-15 months)
Moms on Call: Toddler Book (15 months-4 years)

PARENTING RESOURCES: NEWBORN - 4 YEARS OF AGE

Online Classes:
- Four comprehensive online courses
- Dozens of complimentary videos
- Available via multiple platforms to meet families where they are

One-on-One Consultations:
- Network of trained consultants
- In-home consultations
- Virtual consultations
- Ongoing email support

Mobile Apps (IOS/Android):
- Moms on Call Scheduler
- Moms on Call Toddler by Design

Products:
- The official Moms on Call Swaddle Blanket
- Pacifiers, bottles, sound machines and more!